FRANK McGINTY

TAKE THE
STING
OUT OF
STUDY

Get organized, manage your time
and conquer exam anxiety!

Pembroke Publishers Limited

FRANK McGINTY

TAKE THE

STING

OUT OF

STUDY

Get organized, manage your time and conquer exam anxiety!

Pembroke Publishers Limited

To Carol, Martin, Stephen and Mhari — all very
successful students, but each with their own very
different learning styles and talents.

Pembroke Publishers
538 Hood Road
Markham, Ontario, Canada L3R 3K9
www.pembrokepublishers.com

Distributed in the U.S. by Stenhouse Publishers
477 Congress Street
Portland, ME 04101
www.stenhouse.com

We acknowledge the financial support the Government of Canada through the Book
Publishing Industry Development Program (BPIDP) for our publishing activities.

We acknowledge the Government of Ontario through the Ontario Media Development
Corporation's Ontario Book Initiatve.

National Library of Canada Cataloguing in Publication

McGinty, Frank
   Take the STING out of study / Frank McGinty. -- Canadian ed.

Includes index.
ISBN 1-55138-164-8

   1. Study skills--Study and teaching (Secondary) I. Title.

LB1601.M33 2003   371.3′028′1   C2003-903412-7

Editor   Kathryn Cole, Alison B. Parker
Cover Design: John Zehethofer
Cover Photography: Ajay Photographics
Design: Fielding Design, JayTee Graphics

Printed and bound in Canada
9 8 7 6 5 4 3 2 1

Contents

Chapter 1

Are You a Performing Flea?

There has been a revival of the old fashioned 'flea circuses'. At country fairs people pay money to watch tiny fleas perform circus tricks. There's a tiny ring with ropes, trapezes and unicycles, all cut down to size, and the fleas are trained to perform on them.

Few people find fleas attractive – especially when they're visiting you and won't go away! – but have you ever stopped to consider just how wonderful fleas are? They have no eyes and no wings, yet can jump to 150 times their body length and 80 times their height and land safely. Imagine the human equivalent. You're walking out of the school gates and standing around for a few minutes chatting to your friends. Then when it's time to make your way home, instead of going for the bus, you just flex your knees and soar into the air. Effortlessly you float over the church spire, across the river, and drop safely into your own street. Fleas were born to jump!

In the flea circuses the trainers had to harness all that

energy. It's said that often the fleas were GLUED on to the apparatus, which meant their lives were seriously curtailed!

But what of the fleas that were seen jumping around? Well, the story goes that the trainers put the fleas in sealed jars of varying sizes, according to how high they wanted them to jump. The fleas would spring up – only to bang their heads on the lid. They would try this again and again, each time with the same painful result. After twenty-four hours or so a change would take place. The fleas would jump to just beneath the lid, thereby avoiding the pain. After forty-eight hours the trainers knew they could release the fleas.

The fleas would never again in their lives jump higher than the limit that had been set for them!

What a tragic waste of energy. Yet many of us do the same. We never use more than a fraction of our power because we have allowed others to put limits on us.

Case study: Stella

When Stella was a young girl she loved to go off by herself and sing along with her favorite tapes and CDs. In her imagination she was the singer, performing to a live audience of thousands. But every so often she would break down in embarrassment. You see, her dad had a habit of creeping up unnoticed and watching her with a big grin on his face; then, when Stella saw him, the grin would turn into mocking laughter. Stella would feel humiliated, as if she'd been making a fool of herself.

For years she kept on singing, but only in the privacy of her room and *never* in front of anyone. At secondary school she studied Music and her teacher soon became aware of her great singing voice, but Stella doggedly refused to sing in public. Inside she seethed with resentment as time after time her less talented peers performed at concerts and shows, while Stella just went on hating herself for being so inhibited. Like the performing fleas, Stella's ability had been well and truly clamped.

And she would have stayed that way had her teacher not slowly and gently coaxed and nurtured her talent, for the benefit of everyone.

Change that mindset!

It's amazing how many of the old myths and misconceptions about intelligence are still around today. For example:

- You're born with a certain amount of intelligence and you just have to make the most of it. Right?
- At school some kids are 'brainy' and others are 'dull' and that's just the way it is. Right?

Wrong!

In the old days, people certainly believed these myths. Not only did they believe you could be born a 'dullard', somehow they made it a punishable offence! The offenders were made to sit in a corner of the room, wearing a large pointed cap with the letter 'D' for 'Dunce', and were subjected to physical abuse and ridicule.

So let's bury once and for all the notion that your intelligence is fixed at birth, and that at school you're either going to be 'bright' or 'dull' or somewhere in the middle. Your level of intelligence is *fluid* not *fixed* and there are many factors that can take it up or down in the course of your life. Among these factors are:

- the way you think about yourself
- the skills you learn about learning

Today, more than at any time in the past, success in exams or training courses is considered a necessity. And as the needs of society change, we need to be flexible and confident in our ability to learn new information and skills in order to adapt.

Progress in our thinking

Even children who are born with brain damage or with other limiting conditions can achieve much more intellectually than was ever thought possible in the past. Take Jordan, for example. He is a happy, well-adjusted young man in his early twenties who works in a factory. Take a look at what his mother says about his development:

Jordan has the condition known as Down's Syndrome. I have to admit my spirits sank when they told me all those years ago that my new baby was not 'normal'. But I was determined to do my best for him. You see, I had an elder brother who also had Down's Syndrome.

His name was Donald, and every day my heart would break as he was ridiculed by the so-called 'normal' children. Donald and others with different educational needs were taught in a 'special school', away from the rest. Their bus would pass our school and lots of kids would jeer and laugh. Often Donald would come to the school gates to meet me, and everyone referred to him as 'Daffy Donald'. Believe it or not, they didn't really mean much harm. Many of them liked Donald, but thought of him as stupid or weird. And certainly, Donald didn't learn much in his life. No one thought he had any ability.

Thankfully, by the time Jordan went to school attitudes had changed. Mind you, I still had to fight for the right to have him attend the mainstream school and to have teachers' assistants to help him. You see, I was convinced that it was sheer ignorance that led to the ridiculing of Donald, and I was determined that the other kids should get to know Jordan as a person, albeit a differently-abled one. He had a great time at primary school, and in his teens he split his time between the local comprehensive and a training centre where he learned all kinds of skills. Today, he can look after himself, read, write, organize his finances, use a computer, hold down a full-time job in a factory, go out and about with friends, and enjoy life as a contributing member of society.

Donald, like Stella with her singing, operated within the limits set for him, whereas Jordan was encouraged to explore his capabilities.

There's more to it

So you see, there's a lot more to studying and achievement than simply opening books. It helps to become aware of the limits placed on you by yourself and by others. These can often be quite innocent and unintentional. Maybe your parents have always introduced your elder brother by saying, 'This is Bill. He's the clever one of the family!', for example. And the teaching profession is waking up to the fact that it's not enough to just *teach* a subject and leave the students to learn as best they can. A lot more has to be done to teach students *how* to learn.

Studying and concentration

The techniques of effective study and concentration can seem rather daunting. They include:

- reading at speed *and* retaining what you've read
- organizing information
- understanding concepts
- expressing ideas, opinions and facts, in writing, in speech, in mathematical or scientific formats or in art forms
- using resources efficiently

But these needn't be daunting! There are many tricks of the trade that will help you learn how to learn. The aim of this book is to help you make the most of your intellect by offering very direct advice on how to think about your ability, how to concentrate and how to achieve more in your studies. You will need to develop some personal skills and some emotional insights. But follow the guidelines included in this book and, whatever your starting point, you will be able to raise your performance to a level you probably never thought possible.

Are You a Performing Flea?

Study Tips

1. Be aware of any limits that have been put on you, either by yourself or by others.

2. Change old mindsets about intelligence: it is not 'fixed', as people used to think. It is flexible and can be changed.

3. Even those once considered 'unteachable' are now achieving more and more with modern insights and methods.

Chapter 2

Staying Awake!

Sports Day

Imagine it's Sports Day at school and the runners are lined up for the big race. You'd expect them to be wearing proper running gear so that when they launch themselves from the blocks there's nothing to hold them back or weigh them down. A lot of money and research has gone into designing tops and shorts that reduce wind resistance and allow the athlete's body to breathe. The idea is to cut out all obstacles so that strength and skill comes to the fore.

But in this race (the one you're imagining!), most of the runners are wearing heavy, padded clothes and belts with lead weights around their waists. Instead of carefully designed, lightweight running shoes, they're wearing heavy boots. Two kids, however, *are* properly dressed, and although they're not the fastest runners they cross the finishing line long before the rest.

Why would runners – who, after all, want to succeed –

deliberately handicap themselves like this? They'd be crazy! Yet, if we think of our studies instead of a race, it can be seen that we allow many handicaps to hold us back; it's just that we're not normally aware of them. The 'weights' that hold us back tend to be what is *lacking*:

- a lack of oxygen
- a lack of water
- a lack of rest or sleep
- a lack of appropriate working conditions

The last two items will be considered in more detail in Chapters 6 and 7, but for now let's consider the importance of air and water:

> *I want to learn, but my mind just wanders. No matter how much I try, I just switch off in Mr. Bell's class. At times I've literally fallen asleep. I always get into trouble for it, but I'm more concerned because it's highly embarrassing!*

Some people would give anything to be able to fall asleep during a boring lesson, but for others, staying awake is a serious challenge.

Concentration and staying focused on your work (otherwise known as staying awake!) depend on a number of factors. And these factors are not always what we would normally think to call 'study skills'.

> **Very often your success in concentration will depend on external factors, even on what you do with yourself outside your study times.**

External factors

How can you counteract the tendency to lose interest or fall asleep during a class or personal study period?

The air that you breathe

Derek is a student who suffered in high school from a lack of oxygen in class:

In my first two years at high school I enjoyed Geography, so I picked it as one of my exam subjects from third year onwards. However, I started falling behind and eventually I lost interest. I used to groan every time Geography appeared on my timetable and everyone was complaining about my grades. Words like 'lazy' and 'lack of motivation' appeared on my reports.

I really had to think about this, because I couldn't see a reason for going down in this particular subject. After all, I had enjoyed it in the past. Then I realized what it was. It was more about the room itself than the subject. I had come to hate going into the actual classroom because it was always stuffy and overheated. I would just notice it slightly when I went in, but after about ten minutes or so I used to drift off!

I remember one day the teacher was sitting at the desk giving a commentary on some slides about the Amazon rainforests. The blinds on the window at the front of the classroom were drawn closed so the slides would show up on the white board, but all the other blinds were open and the windows firmly shut. This meant that the classroom became even warmer due to the glare of sunlight through double-glazed windows. We were also breathing recycled air, and could hardly see the slides on the screen. The teacher was one who didn't like to be dis-turbed once started, so nobody spoke up. We just sat there, nodding off!

For successful concentration, fresh air is an ESSENTIAL, not a luxury. At times, even teachers overlook this. The brain, more than any other organ, depends on oxygen and uses a whole 25% of the body's intake. In Derek's class, it turned out that the teacher was simply unaware of the situation. He was so enthusiastic about his subject (which attracted Derek to it in the first place), that he just threw himself into each lesson and overlooked every-thing else. Derek was eventually able to get up the courage to explain the problem after class. The situation was soon corrected.

Many students wake up in the morning with their heads buzzing and the sleepiness dragging them down like a weight on the shoulders – not because they've been overdoing it the night before, but because their window is shut tight and the flow of air in their bedroom is restricted. This is made worse when the bedroom doubles up as a study. How many students do their homework in rooms where even parents fear to tread? The world over, teenagers have notoriously untidy rooms and very often parents give up and leave you to it, don't they? But what happens to your concentration when you're sleeping *and* studying in a room that hasn't been aired, perhaps for days?

Water, water . . .
Research from all around the world points to a dramatic

acceleration in learning when water is taken regularly throughout the school day.

Why should this be so? Well, as you can imagine, there's a very clear link between physical health and concentration. Imagine trying to study with a raging toothache, for example. Many doctors now see a link between dehydration (the effects of a lack of water in the body) and most major illnesses. Most people just don't drink enough water for their bodies' needs. Even in our everyday activities this can have a serious effect.

Case study: Samena

Samena's head was bowed as she slowly trudged along the corridor. She didn't want anyone to see the tears in her eyes, and she didn't want anyone to talk to her.

It was lunchtime, and as she passed the social area in the middle of the school she deliberately ignored her two friends, Nadia and Claire.

'Hmm, there she goes again!' sighed Nadia.

By now Samena was approaching the office. Her throat was dry so she reached into her bag and took a large swig from her bottle of pop before timidly knocking.

'Come in!' called a cheerful voice from inside. 'Oh hello, Samena. Nice to see you . . .'

Mr. Bell, her Guidance Teacher, groaned inwardly. 'How can I help?'

'I think I need to go home, Sir. I'm not well.'

'Again?' asked the teacher incredulously. 'This must be – what? – the fourth time in as many weeks. Did you go to the doctor last time?'

'Yes, but she couldn't find anything wrong with me. They're all quacks! I've always got this headache and I feel so irritable . . .'

'Now, there's a surprise,' murmured Mr. Bell.

'I just can't concentrate and I feel tired – all the time. And I get this horrible feeling in my stomach. One of these days I'm going to throw up in the middle of class. At other times I'm convinced I'm going to have a heart attack.'

'Look, Samena, I want you to see the school nurse. She comes across this kind of thing quite a lot. Let's see if I can get you an appointment right away . . .'

The school nurse at Samena's school had been reading up on the latest studies that suggested the majority of day-to-day ailments in schools are brought about by dehydration. This is caused not only by a lack of sufficient water, but also by an increased consumption of caffeine.

Samena hardly ever drank water by itself. She often felt thirsty, as you do when you have to take sports and PE, and when you're sitting in hot, crowded classrooms. To quench her thirst, Samena had gotten into the habit of drinking lots and lots of pop. To boost her energy, she was a regular muncher of chocolate. Nothing wrong with that, you might say. She's a growing girl, a normal teenager. Right?

Well, unfortunately, no. Samena was becoming both *dehydrated* and *addicted to caffeine*. Dehydration weakens the body and leads to all kinds of weird and unpleasant feelings, including constant headaches. But what exactly happens with caffeine?

Caffeine and its effects

Caffeine is a drug that occurs naturally in some plants and their seeds, and it's added to many foods and drinks. People like to take caffeine because it gives a short-term energy boost. However, it can be addictive and often you have to keep taking more and more to get the same effect. It has also been linked with many illnesses, such as cancer and bone disease. Many people suffer from a condition known as 'caffeine sensitivity', meaning they have more side-effects than the average person. They become irritable, they don't sleep well and they have a rise in their heart rate that can lead to all kinds of problems, such as panic attacks. Caffeine is also a *diuretic*, which means it causes the body to lose fluid – thus leading to further dehydration!

Most teenagers consume caffeine in three ways: in tea and coffee, in soft drinks and in chocolate. You can see now why Samena was in such a mess! She was eating bars of chocolate every day and was drinking four to six cans of pop. She drank very little water and would have at least one soft drink while doing her homework before going to bed. This made her restless during the night, hence her tiredness during the day. Then there was the anxiety because she never knew what was happening to her, compounded by the effects of caffeine, leading to the nausea and heart palpitations. A bit of a mess – but nothing that couldn't be sorted out by following the advice of her school nurse!

Staying Awake!

Many schools now allow and encourage free access to water during lessons. The only drawback has been that this greatly increases the number of students who need to go out to the toilet, but this is a short-term inconvenience, as the body quickly adapts. And the benefits of increased water consumption have been enormous.

But I can't stand water. It's the most boring drink on earth!

This is a regular complaint. But tastes can change. Ten years ago you rarely saw people walking around with bottles of water, but now it's a very common sight, *even in schools.*

So, if you seriously want to improve your concentration, start with this: observe the signs from your body and always keep a bottle of water with you, especially when studying. You may have to make extra visits to the bathroom, but even that extra movement is good for circulation, will keep you awake and help your concentration.

And cut back on the caffeine. Check out these statistics:

Product	Serving Size		Milligrams of Caffeine (approx.)
	oz.	ml.	
Brewed coffee	8	237 (1 cup)	135
Tea (leaf or bag)	8	237	50
Cola, regular	12	355 (1 can)	36—46
Cola, diet	12	355	39—50
Chocolate milk	8	237	8
Candy, milk chocolate	1	28g	7

Values in table referenced from the following sources: Harland, B.F. 2000. Caffeine and nutrition. Nutrition 16(7-8):522–526. Shils, et al., 1999. Modern nutrition in health and disease. 9th Edition. Williams and Wilkins. Waverly Company, Baltimore.

Moderation rules! And if you're daunted by the idea of drinking six to eight glasses of water a day (the amount doctors recommend for young people), then it's good to know that many fruits are about 95% water, particularly grapes, melons, grapefruits and oranges. Pure fruit juices are also a good source of water, and herbal teas (which are caffeine-free) are growing in popularity.

FACT:

MOST Organizations dealing with accelerated learning techniques stress highly the importance of water in the learning process!

Now for some interaction . . .

Many students feel bad about drifting off or even falling asleep during lectures or classes. Yet often it's not their fault. We've seen already that a lack of oxygen or lack of proper hydration might be the cause, but there's another common factor and it has to do with the teaching method. It's now recognized that in a listening situation, concentration wanes after about twenty minutes maximum. But most lectures or lessons go well beyond this. How can you survive?

Use it or lose it

A goalkeeper of a leading soccer team used to dread the games where they were so much in control that he had virtually nothing to do. This was for two reasons. There was always the chance that he might suddenly be called into action and would make a silly mistake, simply because his concentration had gone. And he also knew that the next day in training the coach would put him through his paces for hours on end to 're-sharpen' his skills. It was torture! But he knew the coach was right. It was a case of use it or lose it.

The same is true with concentration in class. You have to work at keeping alert in order to keep your skills finely tuned. So, keep an eye on the time. At about the twenty-minute mark, or even before, if you feel yourself drifting, make sure you do something to **stay involved**. One of the best ways to stay involved throughout a lesson is to take notes (even if the teacher says, 'No need to take notes, I'll be giving a hand-out.'). Even if you never look at your own notes again, it's a way of interacting with the spoken word, a means of keeping yourself involved.

Note-taking can be quite a challenge. The secret is to zero in on the speaker's key points and leave out the padding. So how do you do that?

Keep asking questions!

If you can interact with the teacher and/or others in the class, so much the better. Chip in, make relevant comments and everyone will benefit. Then jot down ideas or information.

But often we're just expected to listen and keep our mouths shut!

You can *still* ask yourself questions – coming up with answers is what true learning is all about. Ask yourself:

Who? What? Why? Where? When? How?

This advice has been given to students for over a hundred years, and it's as relevant today as it was at the start. Answering the Six Questions is not only the best way to keep you awake and involved, it will spark your imagination and help you organize your thoughts.

The answers will be the key points of the lesson, whether it's a spoken lesson or something you are reading. Obviously in some subjects, like Math, there may not be a lot of scope for note-taking. But you can still jot down the elements of a problem or equation while the teacher is explaining it on the board. Then your brain should be fully active when it's your turn to try some examples yourself.

There are different methods of note-taking, and you need to find the one, or make one up, that suits you best.

Taking notes

A very popular form is:

> a heading, with
>> • bullet points, and
>>> – indentations.

Your answers to the Six Questions will give you your first heading. (**What** is the Topic of the lesson? **When** did this take place? **Why**? etc.) Here are some of the notes used for this chapter, laid out in this format:

Staying Awake

- *Concentration*
    - *involves many factors*
    - *some during 'study time'*
    - *others involve 'lifestyle'*
- *Air > Derek*
    - *asleep in geog., low grades*
    - *class struggling, teacher unaware*
    - *no one spoke up!*

- *Air > an essential, not a luxury!*
  - *brain uses 25% of body's oxygen*
- *Water > linked to accelerated learning*
  - *insufficient consumption > dehydration*
  - *> poor health > drop in concentration*
- *Water > Samena*
  - *ill > headaches, tummy, irritable, panic*
  - *caffeine sensitivity*
- *Caffeine*
  - *short-term energy boost*
  - *in tea, coffee, chocolate, soft drinks*
  - *diuretic > dehydration*

. . . and so on.

Note the use of 'white space'. This is not a waste of paper! It relaxes the eye and helps the mind to focus on the main points, which are laid out in a logical sequence. Don't worry if your notes are messy. You can copy them out again when you get home. In fact, this in itself is an excellent way to review.

Later on, in Chapter 4, this plan will be laid out in different ways when we look at specific learning styles.

Now for a fishy story . . .

David gripped his dad's hand tightly as his eyes eagerly swept round the fairground. They had just been watching a medieval battle, where men in chain mail suits of armor had been hacking at each other with swords that were actually bigger than David himself. It was all great excitement for a 6-year-old, and he was now looking for something else to grab his attention.

Passing one of the stalls, something glinting in the sun caught his eye. Hanging from a row of hooks were small plastic see-through bags, each half filled with water. David gasped at the sheer beauty of the objects swimming in the bags – goldfish! 'Uh-oh,' thought Dad, guessing what was coming next. But it was too late! David was already digging deep into his pocket for his spending money.

'There's quite a lot of work in looking after goldfish, you know. You'll have to buy a bowl, and feed them every day and change the water. I don't think your mom will be too pleased . . .' Dad's voice trailed off, as he knew he was fighting a losing battle. David was too busy deciding which ones he liked best.

For the rest of the afternoon Dad had to carry two bags containing a total of four fish, along with David's collection of furry toys, picture books and candyfloss. On the way home in the car all David could talk about was his new-found interest, the goldfish. 'Let's hope it lasts!' thought Dad. He didn't want to discourage David, but nor did he relish the prospect of having to look after four abandoned goldfish himself.

He needn't have worried. As the time went by, David became devoted to the care of his fish. Not for them, life in a tiny cramped bowl! Before long they 'moved up' to a large tank with sand and gravel on the bottom and lots of interesting features like rocks and arches and sunken ships to swim under.

In his teens David took his interest further. He avidly read books and magazines on tropical fish, and he saved up to buy a tank with all the necessary filters, heaters, lights and so on. Before long, he had two tanks that were the talk of the neighborhood. His tanks were carefully balanced with brightly coloured 'top feeders' and 'bottom feeders' and small shoals of tiny fluorescent fish that glowed in the dark. David learned all he could about fish-keeping.

And the next step for David? On to university to study Marine Biology. His lifelong hobby had become a passion. So much the better, he thought, if he could make it his life's work.

At high school, David had not been the brightest of students, but he knew that to follow his dream he would need qualifications in English, Mathematics, Biology and Chemistry. He passed all his exams with flying colors, simply because he was fired up with the secret ingredient of success:

Motivation!

Motivation is the tiny spark that can create a raging fire. David *knew* what he wanted, so although he didn't always enjoy his studies he saw the point of them. And he learned to love them.

If *you* can learn to see the point of your studies, you too can learn to love them. If you dwell on your dislikes, chances are you'll be a reluctant learner. Take an interest! Ask those questions and you'll get involved despite yourself. And once you're involved you'll stay awake! See the purpose, and you'll really take the sting out of studying.

Here are some common complaints from students, followed by some possible remedies:

- *I'm a natural mathematician. I just don't care about literature. Why should I have to study it?*
- *I love reading and finding out about the past. Why do I have to take Math and Science?*
- *It's PE for me. I just want to spend my life in sport. The rest of you can be 'students' if you like.*

The answer is the same to all questions. If you focus narrowly on your 'strong points', you will become a limited thinker. Knowledge is not contained *only* in the sciences or *only* in the arts. To become an all-round, accomplished thinker you must explore the circle of knowledge.

And *that* will make you more employable.

Obviously there are some jobs for which you need a specialized education and training, but even there you will come across as a brighter prospect in interviews and presentations if you can display a more rounded awareness of life.

In many other jobs, however, managers advertise for university or college graduates and they don't really care what their qualifications are. It's the ability to *think* and the *personal resources* of the candidate they're interested in.

It's true that there are a lot of engineers, for example, who know nothing of the arts, but career advisers today stress that *adaptability* is a vital quality, as so many jobs will not be jobs for life. The wider your knowledge base and the more flexible your thinking processes, the more you will have to offer. The studies of Literature, Geography and Graphic Design, for example, all demand very different ways of thinking. The more ways you can master, or at least develop some skills in, the more interests you will be able to develop outside your work. This will not only improve the quality of your life, but will help you cope with career changes should they come your way.

Why not get into the habit, then, of looking at your less attractive subjects this way? Ask yourself, 'What's in this for me?' If, like David, you can get yourself really fired up through something you enjoy, you're on the right track. If you haven't yet discovered the passion of your life, console yourself with the knowledge that you're building up skills for the future. At the very least you'll be more involved in your classes and you'll overcome that mind-numbing boredom everyone meets from time to time.

Study Tips

1. For successful concentration fresh air is an ESSENTIAL, not a luxury.

2. Most people need to drink much more water. Dehydration (the effects of insufficient water) causes a serious loss of concentration.

3. Caffeine – in tea, coffee, chocolate and most soft drinks – can have unpleasant effects, including dehydration, sleeplessness and anxiety.

4. Get involved during lectures: ask questions, make comments, take notes. Find the method of note-taking that works best for you.

5. Get motivated! See a purpose in everything you study/learn. Ask, 'How will this benefit me?'

Chapter 3

Studying With Style

Do you have a preferred learning style? The latest educational theory identifies three distinct styles that play a vital role in the effectiveness of our concentration and study. Yet it would appear most people don't know if they have a preferred style, despite the fact that it affects how we learn and the type of study environment that's best for us.

Are you visual, auditory, kinesthetic . . . or a mixture?

Some people learn best by **looking** at things, others by **listening** to things and others by **moving** around, **handling** things and **doing** things. In other words, three of our five senses tend to be used most in the learning process, and of these three most people have a strong or dominant one.

Visual learners

Because they use their sense of sight more, visual learners tend to use pictures and images rather than words when recalling things from memory. When storing information in their minds they focus on colors, textures, sizes and shapes. They may not remember names, facts and figures, but let them see a face, a picture or a scene and it all comes flooding back. When using their imaginations they 'see' the pictures in their minds, often in very clear detail.

Auditory learners

Noise or sound is important to auditory learners. They love talking and listening, so tend to get involved in conversations and discussions. They can recall words easily from memory, but in their imaginations they tend to *describe* things to themselves rather than see pictures. In language and drama work they love to play around with the spoken word, savoring the rise and fall of expressive pieces and different rhythms, speeds and tones, to suit the meaning. Auditory learning can have other benefits too. For example, Michael is a student who likes to use all his 'spare' time for his studying so that his leisure time is freed up:

> *I've now got one of those radio/cassette players that you can play in the shower, so after my soccer practice I like to play my language tapes while I'm showering. I can transfer the tape to my walkman and keep listening when I'm on the bus or walking home. That way I have to do less studying at night.*

Kinesthetic learners

Feeling and movement are the key things here. Kinesthetic learners prefer not to talk about things or see things in their minds; rather, they like to get right in there and learn by *doing*. Instead of reading about things, they like to explore objects, move things around, put them in order and find out for themselves. Because they are *action* people they can sometimes be slow talkers and very often can't find the right words to express themselves. Yet they *feel* things very acutely on the emotional level, and have a need to demonstrate things outwardly. This sometimes causes difficulties in a society that doesn't understand their needs. And according to educationalist Michael Grinder, many students who drop out of school are kinesthetic learners. This could be because **reading** has such a stronghold on the educational system. Most visual and auditory learners can cope with this (by picturing the scene or picking up the sound of the words) while the kinesthetic learner would rather be doing something else!

Each style has its own pluses and minuses, but it seems that learning takes place most effectively when we use **two or three styles together**. Most people, however, tend to unconsciously develop one style and neglect the other two. This can have serious consequences for your studying!

Case study: Judy

Judy's primary school experience had been varied, to say the least. She had been to no fewer than four different schools. The first change happened when her dad's firm moved him to a different part of the country. Judy didn't settle in at her new school, and she was often teased by her peers. She enrolled in another school in the same area. She liked it, but it was soon noticed that her spelling was very poor and she was slow at reading. Then she was on the move again because of her dad's work, and this time the school reports that followed used the word *dyslexia*, referring to her spelling and reading.

(Note: **Dyslexia** is a language-based disorder where the person has difficulty in recognizing single words on a page. All other development areas, including intelligence, tend to be normal or even above average, but because the person doesn't recognize word formation, there can be a domino effect in the development of spelling and writing.)

Judy was a bright girl, and at her new school, allowance was made for her 'dyslexic difficulties'. Judy's parents and teachers did all they could to boost her confidence in other areas, but it was generally accepted that she would probably never be able to read or spell efficiently.

At secondary school, Judy needed a support programme – someone to read things out and someone to write for her because her spelling was so poor.

Then an amazing thing happened. Judy's class was working on a course called 'Learning Made Easy' and there was a section on making your own 'Learning Passport'. The students had to answer a lot of questions and their overall score gave them an idea of their 'Preferred Learning Style'. Judy's was almost totally auditory, with practically no scores at all in the visual or kinesthetic modes. Further investigations were made and it became clear that Judy had always listened when the teacher or anyone else was reading and she had gotten out of the habit of looking. She was great at following spoken instructions, but couldn't read them for herself. She had come to rely on her auditory style and, as often happens when students have to move from school to school, the development of this limiting habit had gone unnoticed.

What Judy needed now was an intensive course in spelling to train her not only to listen to the sounds of words, but also to look at the patterns of letters and the formation of words on the page. She often discussed with her teacher the similar patterns that she noticed. As her confidence grew, she was able to recognize these patterns in textbooks more quickly and easily, and her reading developed. Over a period of two years, Judy's progress was amazing, and the word *dyslexic* was no longer used to describe her.

This is not to say that Judy totally overcame her challenges, but she may eventually. The term *dyslexia* is often used when there is no progress in reading and spelling after appropriate teaching has been given. Many students in mainstream classes are thought to be 'border-line dyslexics' and make no progress because they feel branded or labelled with a 'condition'. If you or any of your friends fall into this category it's well worth checking out your learning style to see if you are over-specializing in one style at the expense of the others, as

Judy was. Obviously this can have a serious effect on your study and concentration habits.

Case study: Debbie

Debbie had behavioral problems. She was achieving next to nothing at school and her self-esteem was very low. She found sitting still a great challenge, and she was always nudging others, fidgeting with her books and pencils and forever calling out. She bugged every-one, not just her teachers! No one wanted to sit beside her and that just made matters worse.

Like Judy, Debbie was a student who had come to rely on only one learning style. She was a *doer*, not a listener or a watcher. And that didn't suit the way her classes were organized. Most classes started with the teacher giving a talk or demonstration while the students watched and listened. Then it was on to reading from a textbook or worksheet, followed by written or spoken activities. Debbie's poor behavior had sprung from the fact that she got nervous and agitated when expected to listen or read; she wanted to be up and about, touching things, making things and learning about the world that way.

When Debbie's 'Learning Passport' indicated that she was a kinesthetic learner, she got help from a Learning Support teacher (one who assists the class teacher by working with students who have particular needs). Debbie's lessons were restructured so that as far as possible she could be up and moving. For example, she was allowed to do more experimental work in Science; in Math she was taken around the school to work on measurements, areas, ratios and so on; she was allowed to do extra practical work in Home Economics, Drama, Technical Studies and PE.

For the first time in years, Debbie behaved in school and actually started to enjoy her work. She is now being given an individual program to help her become a more visual and auditory learner. She will probably follow a career with lots of opportunities to get about and do things, but she will need the skills and disciplines of the other styles as well if she is to be successful.

Debbie's program was set up to build her confidence and to help her develop the patience to stay calm, slow down and learn to *look* at things, including the written word. She is learning to *listen* more carefully and to follow instructions. There is no easy way to learn these skills, but she benefits from the support and encouragement of her teachers. Life will become easier for kinesthetic learners, not just as they develop their other styles, but as teaching becomes more resource-based. Many subjects in school are moving more and more towards **research**, in which students move around the room to access reference books, CD-ROMs, internet websites and so on, and perform group work.

Perhaps, as Debbie did, you become edgy and frustrated when you're expected to 'knuckle down' to lecture-style teaching. There are other ways to study, but first let's look at the case of Brian who is, in many ways, the opposite of Debbie.

Case study: Brian

Brian dreaded practical work. In PE he was known as a 'Klutz' when it came to shooting hoops, kicking a football or vaulting over the horse. In Science the teacher had lost count of the number of test tubes and measuring cylinders that had slipped through Brian's fingers. And for Brian, Home Economics was a disaster area. He seemed to spend his life apologizing. For as long as he could remember, the words 'You're so clumsy!' rang in his ears. Parents, teachers, friends – they all said it.

Hardly surprising that he preferred a quieter life with his nose in books! It's not that he was a really keen reader. In fact, Brian found reading a challenge, but at least he could get out of the spotlight for a while. When asked to do things, Brian's reactions ranged from embarrassment to outright panic. Even handwriting caused him no end of difficulty.

He found a retreat in the Music department. He couldn't play an instrument, but he loved listening to music and had a great rapport with the Music teacher. Most lunchtimes and sometimes after school, Brian would go along to the Music room, just to listen and sometimes chat about music of all kinds.

It turned out that Brian had a mild form of the condition known as **dyspraxia**. This meant that messages to do with movement were not being fully processed by his brain, so that he found it difficult to judge distances and co-ordinate movements. Since Brian's ability to *plan* an action or activity was affected, he often had problems with his thought processes and was not confident about expressing himself in language.

Dyspraxia affects about 10% of the population, and statistically it will affect about one student in every class of thirty. Boys are four times more likely than girls to have it and it often runs in families.

Because Brian's condition was relatively mild, it was not discovered early in his education. It *appeared* much worse over the years because it was affected by his embarrassment and tendency to panic. For him it was a question of *understanding* his challenge and learning to cope with his negative feelings. He is now working on slowing down when tackling activities and is concentrating on improving his awareness of space. He has been given special exercises to help him judge distances and, as time goes by, his brain is becoming better at processing the messages from his senses.

Brian will learn more and his writing will improve when he brings *movement* into his learning experiences. This *can* be done, and there is plenty of information on living with dyspraxia available on the Internet, or in books and journals – check out your local library. If you feel it necessary, you too can be trained to be more confident in movement. Have a word with your PE or Drama teacher. You could also approach your guidance counsellor or community education department for advice on where to go for help. The benefits will be seen in *all* your subjects.

It really pays to be aware of learning styles and how you are using them. When subject choices have to be made, most schools operate a Core + Options system; that is, there are certain subjects you must study (though there may be some flexibility within that; for example, if you have to take a science course, you can usually choose between Physics, Chemistry and Biology), and there's a list from which you choose other subjects that appeal to you. Obviously, you would have to have a well-developed visual style for Art & Design and a keen kines-thetic sense for PE and Drama, but ideally you shouldn't be restricted in your choices by your dominant style. The more developed *all* the styles are – that is, the more you are used to seeing, hearing *and* doing – the wider the choice you will have.

How many kinds of intelligence are there?

At least eight! And awareness of the different kinds of intelligence is very closely linked to the ideas we've just covered. Your three learning styles are used for getting ideas and information from your senses into your brain, but what you then do with them depends on your intelligences.

Teaching and learning theory is developing all the time and in recent years great progress has been made. (Remember the story about Jordan in Chapter 1, the young man with Down's Syndrome?) For over thirty-four years Dr. Howard Gardner, Professor of Education at Harvard University, has been studying intelligence in many different cultures and societies.

Dr. Gardner notes that schools have tended to teach, assess and reward only two kinds of intelligence: linguistic (words/language) and mathematical. Thankfully things are changing and we now have a greater appreciation of the other forms of intelligence, which are equally important.

Respecting your intelligence

Firstly, if you really want to be motivated, you have to believe that even if you're not a very 'academic' (or 'brainy') student, your particular forms of intelligence are as valuable as any others.

So what are these eight intelligences?

According to Dr. Gardner they are:

- **verbal/linguistic** (speaking, reading and writing)
- **mathematical/logical**
- **visual** (having the ability to see and reproduce shapes, colors, etc.)
- **bodily** (using the body and movement to express oneself, as in sport, drama, dance)
- **musical**
- **interpersonal** (the ability to understand, manage and get along with people)
- **intrapersonal** (the ability to understand yourself, to 'take charge of' and organize yourself)
- **naturalist** (not just the ability to love and appreciate nature, but to sort, classify and recognize patterns in everyday life as well as in nature).

Let's now consider some of the effects awareness of the different forms of intelligence can have on your outlook, and then at how your study sessions can benefit from it.

The 'Remmy Class'

A teacher who has become a great believer in the idea of Gardner's *equally valuable* forms of intelligence tells how it first became obvious to him:

> Shortly after I started teaching, my wife and I had our first child, a boy. At school there was one class I particularly enjoyed teaching, and the students took a great interest in the new arrival. How much did he weigh? What was his name? How was my wife doing? and so on.
>
> Unknown to me, the class got busy and prepared a surprise. One day at the end of lessons they all came trooping over to the staff room with some gifts. I was really touched.
>
> In Art, they had made a beautiful card about 24 inches tall and they'd all signed it. In the technical department, they had made a small garden trowel out of metal and painted it silver and black. In their cooking class, they had made a batch of pastries, beautifully presented in a cake-box tied with a ribbon.
>
> You can imagine how delighted I was when I headed home that evening. To make things even better my parents had dropped by and we invited them to stay for dinner. The dessert went down really well and everyone was greatly impressed by the quality and design of the trowel. My dad in particular couldn't stop talking about it, saying how clever those boys and girls were.
>
> That really got me thinking. You see, those kids were in what was called a 'remedial class'. They had been selected because they had difficulties with language and Math, and were considered less intelligent than average. They weren't allowed to take courses leading to the pub-

lic exams and were known to their fellow-students as the 'Remmy Class'.

They were taught English and Math in their own class-room, and always asked to get out a few minutes before the bell so no one would see them and identify them as 'Remmies'. If they didn't get out early, they used to duck below the windowsill and leave when the yard was clear.

Yet these were kids who, without any prompting, could create attractive artwork, make tools in metal and produce delicious baking – all this as well as teaching us a thing or two about good citizenship! Unintelligent? I don't think so!

The students' skills in the 'practical' subjects were under-valued, and they made little progress in the 'academic' side, because feedback from others taught them to think of themselves as lacking in ability. And this badly affect-ed their self-esteem.

Now contrast that story with the experience of another class, several years later.

The Transition Team

This was a team of young people who were about to experience the move from school to work or further training. Like the kids in the 'Remmy Class', they had not been high-fliers in the academic sense. Yet their school experience had been very different! They (and the other students at school) had been taught to value the different forms of intelligence, so they were confident, outgoing, and took their place easily among the students who were going on to university. Their teacher tells this story:

As a final year project the students took it upon themselves to find out more about the opportunities available to them when they left school, and to report back to others so that an 'Opportunities File' could be built up. This file had the benefit of coming from the students' own point of view, as opposed to that of a teacher or a career officer.

Teamwork was essential. They had to pool ideas, and draw up a list of priorities and an action plan. They decided they would go out to gather information, so phone calls, letters, visits and interviews had to be arranged and carried out. The findings were then presented to the rest of the school in a variety of forms. For example:

- *A video on the life of new students at college was produced.*
- *There was a photographic display on jobs working with animals.*
- *A collage was mounted, showing former students in jobs working with young children.*
- *There was a dance-drama on jobs in the performing arts.*
- *They produced an audiotape with interviews describing life in various shops in a shopping mall.*

Best of all, without any hint of inferiority or embarrassment these kids got up at assemblies and proudly informed everyone about their alternatives to university study. It was very well received!

You will no doubt have noticed that these kids were using all three learning styles – they were moving around, they were using visual and audio images – and they were employing a range of intelligences. It is important not only to respect and value the different forms of intelligence, but to try to *use* them in your daily study routines.

If you can get away from the old idea that study has to be done sitting at a desk with your nose in a book then you will make amazing progress.

Combining your styles and intelligences

When you limit yourself to only one learning style and to only one or two forms of intelligence, you limit yourself to only one or two ways of learning. *Combine* them, on the other hand, and you will not only learn more, but you will learn faster. So how do you do it? Read on . . .

Study Tips

1. Discover your preferred learning style. Do you learn best by looking, by listening or by feeling and doing?

2. Make the most of your preferred style, but also develop the other two and you will learn faster.

3. If you think you may have a specific challenge like dyslexia or dyspraxia you can seek help – but beware of 'labelling' yourself, as this can impose unnecessary limits.

4. Be aware of the eight forms of intelligence. Some are 'practical', some are 'academic'. Value them equally in yourself and in others.

5. By incorporating the various forms of intelligence into your studies you will accelerate your learning and retain more.

Chapter 4

Exploring the Intelligences

Using your intelligences

Let's take **verbal/linguistic** intelligence. Develop your language skills both in speech and writing (e.g., by getting more involved in discussions and keeping a diary every day). This will help you improve your grades in tests involving comprehension or interpretation, such as those where you have to read a passage then answer questions in your own words. Intelligence is all about thinking and understanding, and when you have read a passage, you can then *prove* you have understood it by putting it into your own words. Copy out the exact words from the passage and you'll get few, if any, marks! The more practice you have in using your own words to describe things, the better.

The same applies to all the reading you have to do for your studies. Read a section then ask yourself, 'What was that all about?' 'Who was it about?' ' Where . . . ?' and so on. If you only have a vague idea, go back and read it again and keep working at it. The more your linguistic intelligence is developed, the easier it will be to express the ideas – and the easier it will be to retain them. So you can see why talking with friends and keeping a diary can actually help your reading skills!

If you and some friends have good **interpersonal** skills you can really help one another. As you may know, some schools nowadays have co-operative teaching in classes (that is, two teachers in a class, working together, but each with a particular job to do). Why not start some co-operative learning? Arrange a suitable time and place and help each other, and then:

- Divide the work into sections or topics. Each person can then teach a topic to the others. It's a well-known fact that teaching something is a great way of really coming to terms with it.
- *Discuss* what you have been teaching each other. Trade ideas, notes and opinions. Share your resources; if you have found a brilliant website, tell your friends. They'll then be happy to share theirs with you, and you'll all be better off.

A word of caution, however! Co-operative study will only work if all are motivated learners. Even if you have good intentions, it's very easy to lapse into aimless chit-chat about the latest gossip, music, films . . . which is not the kind of interpersonal intelligence that will help your studies!

How about learning a new language?

If you can speak one language you have the ability to speak thousands! The best way to learn a new language is by surrounding yourself with native speakers. But that's not always possible, so how do you go about learning all those tedious lists of vocabulary?

Use your multiple intelligences and learning styles!

A French teacher volunteered to take a particularly reluctant class, and she had spectacular results. Her 12-year-old students went from hating and dreading their French lessons to enjoying them – and they actually learned some French!

One of the students, Caroline, said, 'The teacher used to say we were not just *speaking* French, we were *doing* French.'

The students had some great ways of learning vocabulary. If they were learning the words for clothes (shirt, shoes, etc.), the teacher would borrow costumes from the Drama department. Each group of students would have an enormous bundle of clothes in front of them. Then, when the teacher called out an item: *une cravate!*, they had to rummage and the first to hold up a tie won a point. Then: *une chemise!* and they all looked for a shirt, and so on.

When it was time to learn the names for animals, the teacher would again call out the words: *un lapin!* and a point would go to the student doing the best imitation of a rabbit; *un chien!* and the class was turned into a pack of dogs! Later the class would write down the words, but not in the normal pencil-and-paper way. They were encouraged to use colors, drawings and diagrams.

One of the boys, Matthew, now a senior student, remembers those early classes fondly:

At first I used to hate French because I found it so difficult. I would look at the lists and lists of vocabulary with the English meanings across from them and hardly any of it stuck in my mind. So I lost interest. Then we went on to the new method with a new teacher and it was great fun. One term we spent weeks preparing a 'French Café' for the teachers at their break. The teachers had to pay to come in and the money went to charity. We learned the words for stuff like tea, coffee, milk, sugar and cake, and sentences like, 'Bonjour, Madame. Bienvenue! Que voulez-vous?' The teachers were a laugh, as most of them tried to speak French too, but we were a lot better than some of them!

Another student, Megan, remembers those lessons too:

Like Matthew, I had trouble remembering the words. But what changed it for me was when the teacher got us to write using lots of colors, and to draw pictures with the French words under them, leaving out the English. I loved doing the drawings – it didn't seem like work! – and somehow the meanings stayed in my head.

You probably noticed the class was using all three learning styles (visual, auditory and kinesthetic), and were employing intelligences such as verbal/linguistic, interpersonal, mathematical (logical) and naturalist (sorting and classifying objects). And it worked for them! They became motivated, they learned much more easily and years later they still retained the knowledge.

Make this work for you too!

What do you do if you want to remember quotations from literature or formulae in Math or Chemistry? Do you sit and repeat them over and over again, thinking that's the best way to do it? That may work; you're using visual and linguistic techniques after all. But why not try to make it *more* visual and *more* linguistic and throw in a few other techniques as well?

One of the best ways to learn poetry, for example, is to copy it out several times, in different styles, different colors, with drawings, shapes and decorations that perhaps represent situations, actions and feelings from the poem. This may sound rather 'cute' or childish, but it's worth remembering that there are two sides to the brain and the Right Brain loves color, humor and images. Learning takes place most effectively when both sides operate together: the Left Brain processes the words, and the Right Brain, the colors and drawings, etc. You'll not only remember the words more easily, you'll find it easier to appreciate the ideas and to form your own opinions. Try it! There's lots of evidence to show that it works!

An equally effective way is to get up, text in hand, and dramatize or recite the piece (yes, out loud!). You can learn particular lines or even those French or German words by mimicking the feeling – sad, happy, excited, angry or whatever. Again, working with others can really pay off here. You can act, improvise or discuss scenes together.

Or why not use your **musical** intelligence? (Again, this is a Right Brain activity.) Put words to music, either to made-up or well-known tunes, but if you're not comfortable with singing, you don't have to sing. By just appreciating the rhythm of words, or the tone, or savoring the rise and fall (the cadence) of the spoken word you're using your musical intelligence.

All these methods will help you get right into the piece, because you'll be asking yourself questions – *and* getting answers – about the mood, the intentions of the author, the meaning and so on.

You can be playful too, either by yourself or with others. You can think up wacky word associations, for example, especially when studying foreign languages, and these will really help the words to 'stick'.

Background music?

Should you have music playing when you study? If it helps, yes! Eerie music in the background will really help you *feel* your way into Shakespeare's *Macbeth*, and romantic music will help you appreciate *Romeo and Juliet*, for example.

But what about when studying other subjects, such as the maths and sciences? Many studies have indicated conclusively that playing baroque music while studying these subjects really helps concentration and leads to improved performance. Other research has indicated that listening to Mozart *before*, not *during* Math study really helps. No one really knows why, but it has been suggested that, because Mozart's music is *algorithmic* (the harmonies present mathematical problems that are solved in a set number of steps), this stimulates the functions in the brain that are used in the study of Math. If you're not a classical music buff, you can always become one! See this as an opportunity to expand your taste.

There's also no doubt that some students perform better with background music of their own choice, whether it be rock, pop, jazz, classical or whatever. But it's not for everyone. James tells this story:

> *I used to go over to my friend Kev's to study. We thought we'd take the teacher's advice and try co-operative learning. But it just didn't work out. We had no problem getting down to work, but I found I just couldn't concentrate. Kev had his stereo playing in the background and it distracted me. We tried working without the music, then Kev said it was no good because the music helped him! We're still good friends, but we do our studying on our own!*

It's likely that Kev was an **auditory** learner and we know that auditory learners are not put off by music; in fact, it often helps them concentrate better, whereas James was probably *not* an auditory learner, so the music was a hindrance. Like Kev and James, you'll need to experiment to find out what works for you.

Keeping on the move

Don't forget the **kinesthetic**. During Math and Science work, get up often and move around. If possible, spend as much time as you can doing things like experiments. You can also write things on cards that can be pinned on a board, and try different sequences by moving them around.

Working with others

Remember your **intrapersonal** skills too. Concentration in subjects such as History, Modern Studies, Drama,

Literature and languages can really benefit from the power of your imagination and inner feelings. Imagine what it would be like to live during the Nazi Holocaust, for example. What would it be like to be a survivor of the concentration camps? When you read about the values and opinions of others, how do these match up with your own? You can actually combine **interpersonal** and **intrapersonal** intelligence. Working with a friend or a group you can each take on a role from a play, from history or from a news story, and discuss your situations and points of view.

This activity, known as *role-play*, is common in Drama classes, but why not transfer it to your homework assignments in other subjects? It will make them much more interesting, as you will question the topic more.

And you will come up with answers and insights that you will retain.

Experiment!

These ideas are just a few suggestions. There are other ways that you can invent for yourself to use your many forms of intelligence and the three learning styles. Perhaps some of the ones described earlier in this chapter won't work for you, but give them a fair try before discarding them. Maybe they would work with a little practice, and you just need to develop them. Or it could be that it's hard to find other people to do the activities with you. Maybe you could raise the idea in class. It would be a pity if you missed out on something that could help you improve your grades!

Note-taking revisited

Let's return to note-taking. Some students find it very helpful to jot down notes using the headings with bullets and indentations style, as described in Chapter 2, both in lectures and when reading a text. These notes can then be transformed by making them more *visual*. You could try, for example:

a timeline

Biography: Elvis Presley

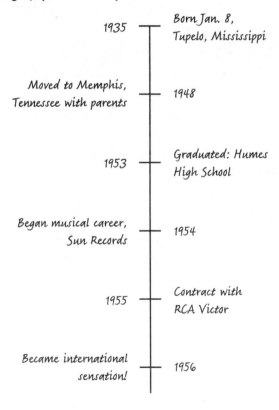

1935	Born Jan. 8, Tupelo, Mississippi
Moved to Memphis, Tennessee with parents	1948
1953	Graduated: Humes High School
Began musical career, Sun Records	1954
1955	Contract with RCA Victor
Became international sensation!	1956

a flow chart

Concentration

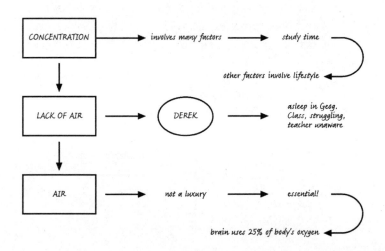

a spider graph

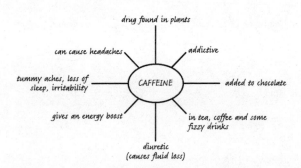

a memory map

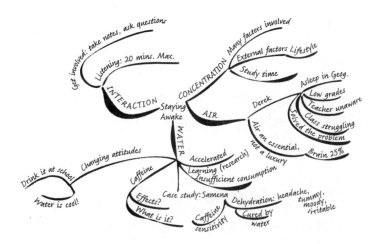

(Compare these methods to the notes in Chapter 2 on pages 29–30 and decide which you prefer.)

These are all forms of **mathematical** (logical) intelligence that can be applied to almost any subject. Some students think they can't do memory maps, but once they work at them, they're amazed at how easy it is to produce them, and they soon appreciate how helpful they can be both in planning and recalling information. However:

> Educational research suggests that not all students find these forms of presentation helpful. No matter how hard some students try to read them, or how positive their attitude, or how willing they are to learn new things, they just seem to find deciphering diagrams a challenge.

You'll never know until you try, but if you *have* tried and they just don't work for you, then stick to the more conventional forms of note-taking. Above all, resist any tendency to feel that because your friends think diagrams are great, there must be something wrong with you. Not true! Do whatever helps you, even if it's different from what others are doing. We're all individuals and we should work out what's best for ourselves.

Study Tips

1. Studying at a desk with your nose in a book has its place, but it's not always the most effective method.

2. Use your multiple intelligences and learning styles to come up with new techniques.

3. Work with friends, use multi-media packages, music, artwork, drama skills – experiment with different forms of learning.

4. Using a variety of approaches and methods will improve your concentration and retention.

Chapter 5

'Go With The Flow' - and Beat That Resistance!

The Flow

Case study: The War of the Worlds

The Head of English approached Room 14 with more than a hint of anxiety. He wasn't sure what he was going to find there. He'd been out of school on a course for the last three days and felt a bit guilty about leaving 2C in the hands of a student teacher for all that time. Normally an experienced teacher would cover on these occasions, but because of staff absences and other commitments there was just no one available. But the student teacher had assured him the class would be fine, and the Vice Principal had agreed to drop by to 'keep an eye on things'.

Nevertheless, 2C were an awkward class. They didn't

seem to like English. 'How can anyone not like English?' the Head asked himself. They were probably giving the student teacher a roasting!

He stopped outside the classroom and was rather surprised to hear . . . nothing! Quietly he opened the door and peeked in. He was astonished to find every student in the room with their heads down, writing feverishly as music played in the background. Seeing him, the student teacher smiled and put her forefinger to her lips, as if to say, 'Don't disturb them.'

'Nice to know who's in charge,' the Head sighed to himself.

'We're doing *The War of the Worlds*,' whispered the student teacher. And the writing continued until a halt was called a few minutes before the bell . . .

The Head needn't have worried. The student teacher had very successfully created the state, which in education, sport and many other activities, including business, has become known as 'The Flow'. It happens when you feel totally engrossed in something creative; you *know* you have the knowledge and skills to cope with the task, so you're firing on all cylinders. You're totally relaxed, and the more you get into The Flow, the more you become unaware of time and effort.

Fly like Canada geese

Maybe you've seen a flock of Canada geese, either in real life or in one of those nature programmes on TV. They can travel great distances in one flight. They expend a lot of energy getting themselves off the ground: they have to hold their wings in a curved position so that the large feathers are pointing down, and they beat furiously to create the lift that will take them up and up. But then, at the right height, they just 'lock' their wings at full span and rest on the fast-flowing air currents. They are carried along almost effortlessly at top speed.

Long-distance runners talk about reaching a similar state, where they feel totally in tune with nature. Many athletes and musicians talk about The Flow: after an initial effort, when they are completely 'warmed up', they reach a state where they just sail along effortlessly.

Back to Class 2C

Class 2C were reluctant writers, because they felt they lacked the imagination and powers of expression for the tasks they were given. Most of them just groaned and 'switched off' when asked to write creatively. But the student teacher caught their imaginations by first of all telling them H.G. Wells's famous story about Martians invading earth. Then she played Jeff Wayne's album, 'War of the Worlds', based on the story. The class enjoyed the story and the music, so the teacher had asked them to write their own version of the story. A tall order. But first, as a class they worked out the bare bones of a plan, the teacher writing the points on the board. After that, the class worked in pairs to polish up their outlines. So by the time each individual started the actual writing they had a detailed paragraph outline laid out in front of them. The background music was put to a vote, and the few who didn't want it were allowed to complete their stories in the school library. The class got busy and loved it!

Too easy! They didn't have to think for themselves. And they all must have produced the same story at the end of the day!

Yes and no. Their stories had the same basic plot, but it's amazing how different they were, as each writer explored his or her individual powers of observation and description and their own use of language. Some highlighted the fighting, others the relationships between the main characters, and others the feelings, such as terror and elation. Once they had the paragraph outlines they had overcome their main barrier, feeling 'stuck'. With a bit of effort to get the assignment under way, they were soon able to get into The Flow.

The Flow is all about overcoming **resistance**: the geese, for instance, have to overcome gravity to reach the high air currents; the athletes have to overcome not only air resistance but *mental* resistance too. And *you* don't need to be told there is *a lot* of resistance to study, learning and concentration!

So how do I get The Flow into my studying?

You know already that tasks have to be sufficiently challenging to keep you from becoming bored, but not overly challenging or you'll become intimidated and put off. The training you receive must provide you with the necessary skills for the task at hand. Much progress, however, is held back or just doesn't happen at all, not because the students aren't working but because they are *trying too hard*. This is where a strong mental attitude comes in. Success comes when you speed up, but, believe it or not, you will speed up by first of all *slowing down*! So what does this mean?

The giant killers!

If you're a soccer fan, you'll know that every year in the Cup competitions there are giant killers: the small clubs, often made up of poorly paid part-timers, who take on and beat the big clubs that have the multi-millionaire 'celebrity' players. The small clubs have nothing to lose; nobody expects them to win, so the players relax and go out to enjoy themselves. Very often, however, the big clubs underestimate the occasion. When things aren't going their way fear sets in: *We're going to be humiliated! We'd better start scoring.* So, they try too hard and they lose The Flow. And when they do this, the goals don't come and, horror of horrors, the part-timers somehow score a winning goal.

A similar thing can happen in education.

Case study: Paula

At school Paula was a high-flyer. She excelled in all her classes, was a talented musician and loved to act on stage in every school production. Yet she had always been a worrier. She had set herself very high standards and it was important to her and her parents that she reached them.

The year before her final exams it all started to go wrong. The first signs were tiredness that very soon led to exhaustion. She became depressed, went into a panic and began to feel alienated and out of touch with everything. She had lost The Flow. And next, she thought, she would lose her sanity.

She became terrified because she thought she was hearing voices and hallucinating. She was losing her grip on reality, and at times didn't know who or where she was. Eventually she became unable to leave home, even to visit her doctor or keep hospital appointments.

It was only when she read a book called *Emotional Intelligence* by Daniel Goleman that she began to claw her way back to normality and eventual achievement.

Part of being **emotionally intelligent** involves being aware of just what is going on in the emotional part of your mind and exercising some control over it. Paula came to realize that her mind was behaving much like the sound system on the stage she loved so much. When a microphone is placed too near the loudspeakers the sound will become distorted, then will rise to an unbearable screech. The feedback continues, creates a whirlpool of sound, and the pitch and volume go up and up.

Paula's negative feelings about her performance were creating a similar whirlpool of emotions. The more she dwelled on them, the more her fears were amplified through her over-active imagination and the worse her mental state became. She was trying too hard. She became nervous and jittery and got herself into a tailspin.

Many students find themselves in this situation. They try too hard, and eventually give in to their fear of failure. This is Enemy Number One of The Flow.

Managing fear is just like managing anger

We can learn here from people like Daniel Goleman who deal in 'anger management'. They tell us that the best way to deal with anger is to strangle an angry thought at birth. Instead of thinking, 'She pushed me and never apologized. She's an ignorant @#?!!', try thinking, 'Oh well, maybe she never noticed me. Maybe she just had some bad news or something.'

That way you keep the levels of **adrenalin** and **cortisol** (chemicals in your body that spur you to anger) in check.

Studies

Fear and anxiety about your studies work in much the same way. The more you *indulge* these thoughts, the more you trigger the chemicals that wind you up.

Are there other ways to stay calm?

The Flow comes about when you are relaxed, confident and on top of things. Start by getting organized! You must keep up with your work in order to have the basic knowledge and skills that will take you up to the 'The Flow Plateau'.

But what if I haven't been studying and have fallen behind?

Come clean! Go to your teachers and explain the situation, and say you really want to catch up and make a go of it. Believe it or not, you'll go a long way before you find a teacher who won't be helpful in this situation. It's very hard to be annoyed with someone who recognizes their faults and genuinely wants to set them right! Listen to their advice, negotiate extensions for assignments and keep the teachers informed every step of the way. Then *they* will stay calm and you'll get the benefit of their support as well as their teaching.

Handling negative feelings

Once you've got things under way you must work on your **determination** to keep going. It won't necessarily be easy, but with effort and practice anyone can do it. Here are some ideas on how to keep yourself on the right track:

- As soon as you feel a wave of panic or fear, take the advice of the famous hypnotist, Paul McKenna. He says that he sometimes feels this fear before speaking in public. He doesn't *deny* it's there (that's most important), but *acknowledges* it and lets it surge through him. Then he simply changes the word *fear* to *anticipation* or *excitement*. This takes the sting out of it and allows him to relax.

  You're in trouble if you try to pretend the feeling of fear is not there! That way, you try to rush past it and you become tense, nervous and panicky. Remember, this is the enemy of The Flow.

- While you're relaxing and thinking about your 'anticipation', you can practise one of The Flow's best friends, rhythmic breathing. When your heart and lungs are relaxed and in control, it sends very positive messages to your brain. Try this popular method of breath control: breath in for three full seconds, hold it for three seconds, then breath out for six seconds. Just try panicking when you're doing that!

- If your mind is taking you along a destructive or negative track about your studies or your abilities, nip it in the bud. Make a determined effort to fill your mind with constructive thoughts. Try using affirmations: short, positive statements you repeat to yourself. There's a lot of evidence that suggests that when such statements are repeated over time, they help not only to keep your spirits up, but also to achieve whatever it is you're after. For example:

'My skills in (whatever) are rapidly improving now.'

'Whatever happens - I'll handle it!'

Turning setbacks around

A survey was taken in a secondary school, asking students who had run into difficulties how they had dealt with the situation. A few said they had sought help, but the vast majority said they had 'switched off' or panicked or got depressed.

A cool head is vital in these situations! What would you do if your assignments were returned with 'Fail' or 'Unsatisfactory' grades? Most students in the survey said they felt like giving up; in fact, many did, while others carried on but with a lot less conviction and no real expectation of success. But these setbacks can be turned around.

As a young child you might have heard this 'wise ' saying:

'If at first you don't succeed,
Try, try, try again!'

This saying really should be reconsidered because it gives the impression that you should keep doing the same thing over and over again until you get it right. It's good to keep trying, yes, but not necessarily in the same way.

Review the situation!

Sooner or later most of us don't do well at something. Believe it or not, students need to have the confidence to fail! When that low test score is announced or the letter 'F' screams out from the page when a paper is returned, it's important that you recognize and acknowledge your reaction. You may feel utterly worthless, but let that feeling run through you, and then instead of wallowing in disappointment, think of it as a spur to take action. Ask yourself:

'What can I learn from this failure? How can I turn this around?'

- You may realize you got the grade you deserved, because you didn't work hard enough.

    Action: Get organized, rearrange your priorities, seek help and catch up.
- You may learn that although you worked very hard, there are some things that you have yet to master and that are pulling you down. For example, maybe you haven't quite memorized the formulae in Math.

    Action: See your Math teacher or a friend. Work on *understanding* the formulae so that it's easier to memorize them.
- You may realize that although you've worked as hard as could be expected, you're making no progress and you have no real interest or motivation in the subject.

    Action: Decide whether or not you need this subject. If you *do* need it, try very hard to take an interest in it; consider the potential benefits the course may offer.

    If you don't need it, then renegotiate your courses. If they won't let you give it up because it's too late to change, then realize that taking an interest will not only make it more pleasant for you, but will make you learn more than you otherwise would. Everything you study at school should be **within your interests, your capabilities and for your benefit.**

So *try, try, try* again by analyzing your performance and mistakes positively, then taking the necessary action. If you have genuinely tried to get into The Flow, but find yourself constantly buffeted by the wind, then rest assured all is not lost – it's just that you've not got yourself properly aligned. Some **redirection** may be required. You might benefit from talking to a teacher, counselor or career adviser. With a cool head and confident attitude you will be able to make the necessary adjustments in your courses and, if necessary, in your study habits.

Study Tips

1. At all costs, avoid the trap of trying too hard.

2. Learn how to relax.

3. Learn the techniques of managing fear – this will prevent the build-up of anxiety.

4. Handle potentially destructive feelings by practising positive self-talk.

5. See 'failure' simply as a call to take a different course of action (e.g., work harder, seek help, renegotiate courses, get and stay organized).

6. Follow the suggestions in this chapter to get into The Flow (that state of 'sailing' through your studies almost effortlessly and enjoyably).

Chapter 6

There's a Time . . .

The previous chapter covers the importance of not taking your studies too seriously – but if you want to succeed, it's equally important to give them the attention they deserve! It's a question of **balance.**

The show must go on!

This slogan goes way back to the early days of live theatre, and it's one you still hear today. Actors, singers, dancers – performers of all kinds – were expected to turn up and entertain, no matter what their personal circumstances. The philosophy was: *'It doesn't matter if you're exhausted, if you've just lost someone special or if your relationship has just broken up; you're the star and it's you the public have paid to see. Get out there and give the performance of your life!'*

Many a stand-up comic has gone on stage with a breaking heart, yet has managed to have the audience in stitches. While you might admire their courage, you might also wonder whether 'pressing on regardless' is the best response. The fact that showbiz is littered with an above average rate of suicides, breakdowns, failed relationships and addictions suggests that perhaps it's not.

Rest

A symptom like sadness or energy loss is nature's way of telling you to withdraw for a while in order to rest and recuperate. Very often these symptoms are ignored and we 'press on regardless'. However, if rest and recuperation haven't taken place, depression often sets in. This sometimes prompts the sufferer to look for artificial stimulation in order to keep up the appearance of normality; and very often this is medication, drugs or alcohol. This happens in all walks of life, but there is growing concern about the number of students who are succumbing to these pressures. In Chapter 2 it was mentioned that success in concentration depends not just on what you do during your study times, but on what you do at other times too. What you need is a balance between your study and other areas of your life.

Striking the right balance

A good night's sleep

Chapter 2 covered the importance of **water** and **air** for concentration, but a vitally important aspect that's often overlooked by young people is a **good night's sleep**! Parents and grandparents go on and on about it, so it's something we tend to nod politely about – then ignore. After all, you're only young once and, anyway, you know from experience that you can party till the small hours and still handle your classes next day. All your friends do it too, so it's no big deal.

But although you may not actually *feel* tired, medical experts insist that the brain's ability to perform thinking, reasoning and recalling skills are greatly reduced when it hasn't had sufficient recovery time (i.e., sleep). And for young people, sufficient recovery time takes, on average, around eight hours per night. It's worth asking yourself whether the reason you have difficulty remembering things, or you just can't seem to get going when you have that essay to write, or all that Chemistry stuff remains a mystery – might be *not* because the work is too 'hard', but because your brain is just not ready for it. Artificial stimulation – caffeine, alcohol, a sugar 'fix' or even drugs – only makes matters worse in the long run.

Getting to sleep at a reasonable hour obviously requires determination – switching off that TV late at night can be a major challenge! But once you feel the pay-off it will become a lot easier. Remember those Canada geese in Chapter 5? It takes **effort** to get into The Flow.

Looking ahead

Taking the time for sufficient sleep is all part of being organized, and another part of being organized is **forward planning**. If you master this you'll really benefit, not only in your studies, but in your life in general, as you'll be more relaxed and content and in charge of things.

It's a good idea to keep some sort of diary or planner to record your term's activities, including when homework assignments are due, when assessments and exams will take place, which days are holidays, which are study days and so on. Seeing the 'big picture' stops the nasty things like class tests from creeping up on you unawares. (And they are only nasty when you're not ready for them!) You can also record things such as medical and dental appointments, meetings with teachers and organized events like Drama practice, games and study sessions with friends. By planning ahead and keeping on top of things, you avoid getting stressed over forgetting things or leaving things to the last minute.

You can also include your results and grades in your planner, plus comments so that you can see what type of pattern (good or not so good) is building up. If it's a good pattern, it will encourage you to keep going and you'll enjoy it. If it's not so good it will encourage you to take action! Many teachers advise students to record comments of their own, and positive self-talk can work wonders for your confidence and motivation. Once you get into the routine of mapping out your study activities you really will enjoy the experience, because it is both:

- **relaxing** – it helps keep worry and anxiety at bay, as you can see ahead and work *towards* an event, and

- **creative** – working towards a goal and charting your progress can be very satisfying.

A wall-chart planner & study timetable
Over periods of exams or assessments many students find it helpful to have a plan of action for the weeks ahead. This works in a similar way to the diary/planner, but it involves *two* things:

- Recording on a **wall-chart** the actual days when

you have an exam and the number of days in between exams. For example, you may have Physics on Monday, English on Tuesday, then nothing until Math the following Monday. Tuesday and Wednesday after that may be free, then German, Physical Education and History all come in quick succession with no free days between them. (Note that the timing of your exams is a matter of luck: you may have yours evenly spread over a number of weeks, while your friend may have a slack period followed by a fairly dense couple of weeks.) Seeing this laid out on your wall-chart helps you plan time for the review of all subjects so that you're not caught short if there's a pile-up in the middle or at the end. You can also sometimes plan to have the odd day off in between times when you do relaxing things and don't even give your exams a thought.

- A **study timetable** involves planning what you do on review days to get the most out of them – and that does not mean studying all the time! (And remember, there are other ways to study than 'nose-in-books'! Use those learning styles and multiple intelligences! – see Chapters 3 and 4). Many people find it helpful to think of morning, afternoon and evening sessions, with two sessions for study and one for leisure. For example:

  - Monday morning could be a meeting in school with friends to help each other with language work. In the afternoon you could go shopping or go for a swim with those same friends, then in the evening you could practise some Math at home on your own. Notice that you have not only built in a leisure period, but you've studied subjects that make different demands on your brain (Language and Math) and you have built in different methods of study.

- Tuesday, you could sleep in then watch a video. After lunch it's to school for some extra help from your Music teacher, and in the evening you're reading over your History notes. But whether your evening session is a study or leisure one, you should, of course, allow for your eight hours' sleep!

• Always try to build in some fairly demanding physical exercise sessions. Exam periods are potentially very stressful, and exercise is a great way to work off pent-up nervous energy (and brings many other health benefits too).

• Here's an example of a study timetable:

WEEK BEGINNING: Mon. 25 June			
	MORNING	AFTERNOON	EVENING	NOTES
MON	School 9.30 Revise German (see teacher)	Fitness centre: swimming	Home Go over Math formulae	Rent video on way home!
TUES	Sleep in Watch video	School 2.00 Music practice	Home Review History notes	Return video on way home

. . . and so on

Coping with your parents

Now for a common complaint. After a few days parents will have noticed you going to the cinema during a 'study afternoon' or going out dancing during the exam period. The vast majority of parents have their children's best interests at heart, and they become very uneasy when they see this. They're thinking: 'You can't possibly be making the most of your revision time sitting around in the middle of the morning watching videos or DVDs!'

When parents are anxious it's easy for them to overlook the other two sessions that day when the hard work is put in! But assure them that three study sessions a day during exam periods is not only undesirable, it can be *damaging*. It's about maintaining balance and allowing body and brain to pace themselves efficiently. The need for QRT (Quality Recovery Time) is well recognized by psychologists and medical authorities and the benefits of it are increased productivity and performance, health and well-being. Many parents do misunderstand this, so put their minds at rest by letting them read this AND by showing them your timetable and wall-chart ahead of time. Keeping them well informed will benefit everyone.

Two parts study and one part rest is an excellent ratio for avoiding burnout AND for increasing your chances of success.

As always, a word of caution!

Having a routine for your studies is a great idea. However, it's important that you are flexible and see yourself as the *master* not the *slave* of time.

Case study: Amna

Amna was desperate to study Medicine at university. Ever since her early childhood in Sri Lanka she had been aware of the need for improved medical care in the land of her birth, and she wanted to be part of that. She was glad her parents had emigrated because it meant she could have a good education and train to be a doctor. She intended to work for some time in her adopted country, then go back to Sri Lanka and devote her life to those who needed her help most.

In her final year at secondary school, the exams that would decide her future loomed closer and closer. She'd followed her teacher's advice and drawn up a study plan, and was following it to the letter. So far so good.

But two weeks into her study program, she started feeling the strain. She couldn't understand why. There was just a heaviness in her approach to work, a slug-gishness every time she tried to get down to it.

One Friday, Amna got up at 7:00 a.m. According to her study plan she should be at her books by 8:00 a.m., working through the morning until lunchtime. So at 8:00 a.m. precisely Amna sat down at her desk and opened her books. Five minutes later she sighed out loud, then hoped her mother and brother, who were by now rustling around in their rooms, hadn't heard her. She stared into space for a moment or two, and a smile slowly spread across her lips. 'I know!' she said. And with that she went back to bed, curled up, and was fast asleep in minutes.

She was woken up at 10:00 a.m by her mother anx-iously shaking her shoulder. 'Amna! Amna! Wake up. What about your studying? You're losing precious time! Are you not well?'

'Don't worry, Mom, I'm fine,' replied Amna through a haze. 'I know what I'm doing. I'll explain later.' And with that she turned over and went back to sleep.

Her mom went downstairs, thinking to herself that it was so unlike her daughter to waste her time lying around in bed when she should be studying. And she wasn't unwell . . . What could she be thinking of?

At 12:40 p.m. Amna woke up, stretched and looked at the revision chart pinned above her desk. 'Back to the drawing-board!' she said to herself. 'A few adjustments required . . .' And instead of feeling guilty or angry with herself, she felt a renewed energy and confidence. She had just taught herself a very important lesson!

Amna had been keeping faithfully to her study regime and was making excellent progress. She felt in charge, anxiety was being kept at bay – but over the last few days of her timetable an inexplicable weariness had come over her. Just in time, she realized what it was: **fatigue**. At first she couldn't explain it; after all, she was following all the advice about sleep, fresh air, drinking water, taking breaks, etc., but there it was nonetheless. So what did she do? She took positive action by going back to bed, which did two things: it refreshed her because, for whatever reason, she needed extra sleep that day, and it boosted her confidence and determination as she demonstrated to herself that *she*, not the study plan, was in charge. By listening to her inner voice she taught herself to be flexible and adaptable, and by doing so, solved the problem. Amna is now at university studying Medicine and all is going according to plan.

Like Amna, you may decide that you need extra sleep one day, but equally, you may decide that going for a walk, going shopping or meeting friends for a movie is the best solution for a particular occasion. Whatever you decide, keep to the general plan of action:

- Get into the habit of using a diary/planner.
- Create a wall-chart with exam dates and a study timetable.
- Follow your plans in a disciplined and positive way.

BUT

- Should the need arise, have the confidence to be flexible and adaptable.

How serious are exams?

Two groups of people who tend to take exams *very* seriously are parents and teachers, the first because they want the best for their children and see exam success as the best way to gauge this and move forward. And the second group want the best for their students too, but they have the added complication of having their reputations depend on their students' results. This means that almost as soon as students enter secondary school many come under a two-pronged attack! As one student put it: 'I've only just got here and already the teachers and my parents have got me terrified of the exams. You'd think my life depended on it!'

But your life doesn't depend on it. In fact, there was a very tragic case a few years ago that might help get your thoughts about exams into perspective. A young man

was attending a family gathering to celebrate his gradu-
ation from university. His school career had not been
without its challenges, but he had worked hard to overcome them and eventually proceeded to university. His
family were both delighted and proud when he graduat-
ed. But that very night, on his way back to his flat, he was
killed in a car crash. His college friends who attended the
funeral felt a huge sense of loss and a total inability to
comprehend his death. They couldn't understand why it
happened just at that time, after he'd worked so hard to
get where he wanted to be. One of the students said: 'I'm
halfway through my Honors degree course, and the past
two years have been hell. I've two more years to go and
I'm going to do my best – but after this there's no way
worry is going to get me down again. Life is for
living, not worrying.'

One teacher who conveys this philosophy to his students
sometimes gets complaints from parents, and his col-
leagues:

*Over the years I've seen so many able students floun-
dering because of pressure put on them by others. As
well as the burden of their heavy workload, they're carry-
ing the stress of expectations: they want their parents to
be proud of them; they want to please their teachers;
sometimes they feel they must compete with classmates.
They live with the fear of losing face should they fail.*

*I often tell them exams are not all that important! In the
grand scheme of things, there's a lot more that matters!
I tell them to throw the whole anxiety thing out the window: no one should be motivated for exams by a fear of*

failure. They should work to their ability in order to develop themselves. If they've done their best and they pass, that's fine. If they've done their best and they fail, that's fine too. With the right amount of confidence, they will always find something else and the great adventure of life will go on. And do you know what? Once they get their heads around this, it's amazing how well they do!

The message:

Keep things in perspective and you won't crumble under pressure.

Study Tips

1. *Success in study and concentration depends on more than 'getting down to your work' – it depends on striking the right balance between studies and other areas of your life.*

2. *As well as providing yourself with water and fresh air, make sure you get sufficient sleep and rest. You may not feel tired, but fatigue can manifest itself in many other ways.*

3. *Develop the habit of forward planning. Keep a study diary and refer to it frequently!*

4. *During exam periods use a wall-chart and a study timetable to help keep on top.*

5. *Be flexible. Be the master, not the slave of time.*

6. *See exams as useful rather than vital. Keep things in perspective.*

Chapter 7

. . . and a Place!

There's one activity that really gives students with new-found determination to throw themselves into their studies a boost: organizing a comfortable workspace with all the knick-knacks that go with being an organized student!

It should be pointed out that not all students work best at a desk. We've seen already that studying can be done in lots of different ways. What works for most people, however, is creating or using a place that you *associate* with study. It can be a corner of your bedroom or even your dining room table, but you should have easy access to it and somewhere to keep supplies at hand. Many students become reluctant when they have difficulty finding everything they need, and when books and materials are stored in lots of different places. There's an old saying: 'It's a day's work getting started.' If your stuff isn't easily at hand you're going to find it all the more difficult to get going.

The essentials for a good study space

A good study space must be comfortable, well-heated and well-aired.

There should be proper lighting too. Research indicates that it suits most people's eyes best if the light source is on the left. If you're studying with natural light it's better if your desk is not facing your window, as this creates glare; better to have it side-on to the window so that the light comes from the left and there's no shadow to block it. When you're using artificial lighting, the two recommended forms are an uplighter (which casts the light upwards to the ceiling and from there it 'floods' over the entire room) and a desktop reading lamp. This ensures sufficient light for reading, cuts out shadows and reduces glare. Uplighters can be bought very cheaply and they're well worth the investment because they contribute to your health and comfort. Desktop lamps are handy as they focus the light on to your work surface, and they can usually be adjusted to prevent glare and eliminate shadows.

Next, get yourself some of those knick-knacks! – a variety of pens with different colored inks, plenty of pencils (preferably with erasers attached), ring-binders, a punch for making the holes in your pages, polythene pockets, a stapler and staples, rulers, text highlighters, sticky neon markers . . . You can really go mad on a visit to your local school supply store with a Christmas or birthday gift voucher! Once you've got them all gathered, keep them in their place so that you can always find them.

The number-one obstacle to efficient study?
Having to ask, 'Who's got a spare pen?'

. . . and a Place!

The secret is to have somewhere that you *associate* with study, and when you go there you automatically go into 'study mode'. And everything is there where you left it, just waiting for you to get back! Suppose you're halfway through an accounts assignment, for example, and you have to leave it. The next day, or whenever you get back, it will be much easier to pick up the threads again if your books are still open at the relevant pages and your notes are all laid out on your work surface. 'Study mode' will just click in! On the other hand, if your books are all over the place (some in your bag, some under your bed . . .) and you can't find any notepaper, let alone a pen to write with, you're going to be severely challenged – the latest episode of your favorite TV soap is going to be all the more appealing!

But I don't have a workspace. There's no room for that in my house. It's not my fault!

That's regrettable, but it's a challenge that *can* be overcome. Kieran had to face this very situation:

I come from a big family and there's not a lot of room at home. I want to be a computer programmer, so I need to get good grades at school to qualify for university. I tried studying at home, but it just didn't work out. You see, I have to share a room with my two young brothers; my bed's at one side and they have bunk beds along the other, so there's no room for a desk or table. Even if there were, it still wouldn't work out because they're always shouting and climbing all over the place. I can't blame them, they're just kids; but it would be impossible to concentrate in there.

Downstairs is no better. Something always seems to

be going on in the kitchen, and Dad has the TV blaring in the living room. There's just nowhere for peace and quiet.

This type of situation is more common than you might think. In another home there may be a lack of central heating, and in another, maybe unhappiness and fights. So what can be done? Kieran found an answer:

A few of us approached our teachers and a homework club was set up. This was a bit different from the after-school Supported Study scheme that was already running. The club is designed for those who, for whatever reason, can't work at home, whereas the Supported Study goes over points made in class or just gives extra practice, and the homework still has to be done at home. The club meets every night after school and on Saturday morning. Some even come into school early before it starts, which helps those who are playing team games like football after school, or those who just want to go out with their friends.

Most members have a locker to keep their things in, but if there aren't enough lockers you're given cupboard space. This means all your books and stuff can be gathered and kept safely in the one place. You don't ever have to take them home, because you aren't ever studying at home. It's worked out really well. I wish I could have my own place at home, but this is the next best thing.

If despite all your efforts you still haven't got a study base, or you're not interested in joining a club, why not gather all your knick-knacks and materials together and keep a travelling pack? Take it to your local library, use a room in a friend's or relative's house, or even stay behind after school and work on your own. This situation is not ideal, but it's another challenge that can be overcome. Success will be all the sweeter when you eventually taste it!

Another helpful aspect of the homework club is the **mutual support** it offers. This suits kids who attend not because they don't have a space at home, but because they find it extremely challenging to get down to work on their own.

Case study: The Polar Bear Swim Club

It was the 1st of January, New Year's Day, at the shore of English Bay in Vancouver, BC. The grey clouds hung in the sky as a light drizzle fell. Yet the happy crowds of some thousands of people gathered seemed not to notice as they laughed and chattered on the beach.

There were men, women and children of all ages, not just from Canada, but from all over the world. Over a thousand of those present were in swimwear, while many in the crowd were decked out in costumes: polar bears, of course, as well as clowns, Vikings and superheroes.

An expectant hush fell over the crowd as renowned blind athlete Ivy Granstrom approached the water to begin the festivities. At 91 years old, the 'Queen of the Polar Bears' was celebrating her 75th New Year's dip into the icy waters of English Bay. Cheers and accolades rose from the crowd as Ivy returned to the beach and the main event began.

1200 swimmers dove into the waves, today merely a chilly 8°C (46°F) — the coldest swim on record took place in 1985 at a frigid 3°C (38°F) — brrr! As the first swimmer reached the 100 yard marker buoy, winning the annual race, others swam and splashed around before heading back to the beach and their waiting towels and mugs of steaming hot chocolate.

This was one of Vancouver's traditional New Year's celebrations, known as the Polar Bear Swim. An annual event since 1920, no one has ever recorded any accidents, or even so much as a cold. Why not? This success is probably due to the bulwark of mutual support from the hundreds of swimmers, as well as their admiring audience. Can you imagine what it would be like standing *by yourself* on the freezing beach in the middle of winter and gathering your courage to jump in, then scrambling out to find your own towel? And all just for fun! It's a very different experience with the support of the crowd behind you.

It was the same kind of encouragement and support that went on in Kieran's homework club. A workplace was made available, storage facilities were supplied and there was regular encouragement from teachers *and* fellow students. Like the polar bear swimmers, the club members seemed to overlook the 'pain' and got on with it.

Culture
Much depends on the culture or 'ethos' (the prevailing attitudes or ideas that influence how a group behaves) of the group you find yourself in. If, like Kieran, you can

counteract your challenges at home with the support of a group, then make the most of it. But if the culture is very much *against* achievement and studying is just *not cool*, then you really have to be strong. Going against the crowd is not easy, and often people prefer to follow like sheep.

The laughing shepherd boy

A young shepherd boy long ago used to lead his flock down from the pastures to the pen every night. He would open the gate and, to amuse himself, would hold his stick horizontally about one metre above the ground across the opening. The first few sheep would have to jump over the stick to get into the pen, then the boy would quickly pull the stick away. He would stand back and laugh as the other sheep arrived at the gate and jumped over thin air. There was no longer a barrier, so there was no need to jump, but they did it anyway because all the rest before them had done it!

The 'herd mentality' can be equally strong in humans. Sometimes it can act as a great advantage and support in our lives. At other times it can be destructive.

If you find you have to stand up against your friends or the crowd in order to take your studies seriously, then you will need the qualities and skills of confidence, self-assurance and assertiveness. You can develop these on your own – by reading books, listening to tapes or taking courses that deal with these topics – but it would be much easier for you if you had the support of a group of like-minded people. If there are no initiatives like home-work clubs or supported study sessions at your school,

... and a Place!

then why not take the initiative yourself? Ask your guidance teacher, counsellor, director of studies (or whatever
the professional support in your school is called) for help.
There are probably more kids in your school who would
appreciate this than you imagine. Do them all a favor!

Study Tips

*1. Make sure you have a comfortable, heated, well-aired and
well-lit workspace. At home, at a friend's/relative's, at school
– it doesn't matter where, but get one!*

*2. Equip yourself with all the materials you need: notepads,
binders, pens, pencils, etc. – these promote efficiency.*

*3. If working on your own is a serious challenge, organize a
study group with your peers where you can support and
encourage each other.*

*4. If studying means going against the culture of your group,
be assertive and take the initiative!*

Chapter 8

Back to Basics

Effective reading and writing

It's been stressed throughout this book that for accelerated learning to take place it is important to get into the habit of learning in lots of different ways: through physical movement, by using music and art, by using scientific skills, by speaking and listening to others and so on. Much will still depend, however, on the traditional means of studying: reading and writing. These two means of communication form a large part of any student's workload, so this chapter is devoted to brushing up on reading and writing skills.

It's like painting a wall

Question: What do reading and painting a wall have in common?

Answer: Once is rarely enough.

Suppose it's autumn and the leaves are beginning to fall. The days are becoming shorter and there's a slight nip in the air. Gone are the long, balmy days of summer . . . and your parents' homing instinct is awakened! Let's batten down the hatches before winter strikes! The bad news is that they want the house spruced up before Aunt Jean arrives for the Christmas holidays and casts her critical eye over the decor. Everybody has to pull their weight, and for you that means painting your bedroom.

If you're like most kids, first of all you'll protest. Then when you realize there's no escape, you'll be convinced that a quick once over is all that's needed. Down come your posters, the furniture is shifted and out come the drop sheets. Round you go with your paintbrush or roller in double quick time. 'Finished!' you say to yourself. 'A work of art!' But Mom doesn't agree.

'It's too patchy!' 'It's too thin' 'I can see the color under it' 'It's streaky!' . . .

Well, it was worth a try – and if you're honest, you'll admit Mom is right. So off you go again – only this time it spreads much more easily and it doesn't take so long. The second coat looks really good too – it's all evened out and there's not a streak to be seen. If your mom's really fussy, though, she may want a third coat, especially if the previous color was very strong and she's convinced she can still see shades of it here and there. But in the end it's all been worth it.

Believe it or not, reading is something like that. One coat (or one reading) is rarely enough. Many students overlook this point – they read a text once only, then all their opinions and comments are based on that one scanty reading. Like the first coat on the wall, their understanding of the text is probably patchy; some parts may have been covered fully, but there are gaps in others. What's needed is a second coat. And just as the second coat went on more easily, so the second reading will be easier and quicker, and more will be retained and understood. If it's a particularly heavy text, a third coat – sorry, reading! – might be necessary.

This is important even in exams. But instead of taking the time to calmly read over a passage several times before attempting a written answer, someone always gets busy with pen and paper too quickly. Then another, and another, and before long everyone is at it. It's the influence of the group, following each other just like the sheep in Chapter 7. Just because they see the others jumping in, they think they'd better get under way too, so the reading suffers.

Chill out! Just as you prepared your room for painting (by taking down posters, etc.), you should **prepare** your reading by first of all **scanning the text**. If it's a book, look at the cover and read the blurb (the part, usually on the back or the inside cover flap, that sums up what the book is about). Check out the list of contents, flick through the pages and look at headings or diagrams and illustrations. If a particular sentence or paragraph catches your attention, skim over it quickly. Doing this may take a little time, but it **speeds up** the reading process, so you not only save time, but it helps you take in more. How does it do that? Well, it gets your Reticular Activating System (RAS) in gear!

What on earth is my Reticular Activating System?

It's a small clump of cells at the base of the brain stem and it monitors the millions of stimuli that come in through the senses. It decides what's important and should therefore be passed to the conscious mind, and what's unimportant and should be passed to the subconscious.

City life

It took Karen a long time to settle into her new life at university. All her life she had loved animals and couldn't wait to get her veterinary training under way. She was a brilliant student, she had a pleasant, outgoing personality and was confident and comfortable in the company of others. She had expected to take to university like a duck to water. So what was the problem?

In a word, traffic. Karen had grown up in a rural setting on the East Coast. She had lived on a farm with her brothers and sisters next to a small village, and every day, with the other local children, she was bussed to the local high school up the coast. The pace of life was slow, people tended to be laid-back, and although she'd visited big cities many times, it came as a shock when she actually had to live in one.

The constant noise and fumes were hard to take – the screeching of brakes, the roaring of buses as they dragged their way in and out of the traffic lanes, the smell of diesel mixed with petrol exhaust – all this was a long way from the easier pace of life back home. Yet to her new friends, who had lived in cities or large towns all their lives, this was merely background activity. They hardly noticed it at all, and many of them couldn't really understand why it was such a big deal to Karen.

Eventually, however, a change took place. Not in the traffic, but in Karen's perception of it. Nowadays she can walk through the streets and, like the others, she hardly bats an eyelid. Her Reticular Activating System is working well! At first the noise and bustle of the streets were perceived as an irritation, so her RAS flagged it up to her conscious mind. As the months went by, however, Karen adapted and realized she could live with it. Her RAS sent it to her unconscious and it was no longer considered an irritation. And Karen is now hardly even aware of the things that once annoyed and worried her so much.

Much the same happens when a weird piece of sculpture or a new building with an unusual design appears in a public space. At first there's curiosity, irritation or even outrage, then in time people hardly even notice it.

The RAS and reading

When you're reading for pleasure and relaxation you don't need an active RAS, but when you read for information and understanding it can be really useful. Here's how to get your RAS up and running. Before you read your text ask yourself questions similar to the Six Questions we discussed in Chapter 2. For example:

- **What** do I want from this text?
- **What** is this piece of writing about?
- **Who** is the author and **who** is it intended for?
- **How** can this writing help me?

- **Where** in the text can I find the specific details I need?
- **What** is the author's point of view?
- **How** is that view put across? Is it by being serious? logical? funny? witty? sarcastic? . . .
- **What** type of language is being used? Is it formal? scientific? informal? slang?
- **What** effect does this have on me? **How** do I feel? **How** do I respond to it? With pleasure? anger? sadness? compassion? fear? . . .
- To **what** extent do I agree or disagree with the writer?
- **How** successful is the writer's technique?

And so on.

Then, as you scan the text (that is, flick through it, looking at headings, illustrations, diagrams and anything that stands out or otherwise catches your eye) your RAS will be on the lookout for answers. When you get down to the actual reading, the RAS is well primed and will send all the relevant details to your conscious mind. Many students don't do this even when they know about it, either because it seems too simple or they lack the patience (or the nerve in an exam hall!) to take the time. Yet it's a tried and tested method and is known to work well. It is another case of **slowing down** in order to **speed up**.

The questioning technique is particularly useful in exam papers, in which you have to read a text, then answer by:

- extracting information
- giving your own opinions on facts or ideas expressed in the text

- evaluating the author's work (i.e., commenting on the style, use of language and how ideas and opinions are presented).

The more you question things before and during your reading, the more your RAS will come to your assistance! This will improve your study habits, your concentration span and your learning.

Clear writing

Much the same applies to your writing. When you have a specific task to do it would help to ask questions so that you are absolutely clear in your mind what you are setting out to do. See the 'big picture' clearly in your mind.

- **What** exactly is the purpose of my task? (Note that the purpose may be *real*, as in writing a letter of complaint to a newspaper, or it may be *imaginary*, as in writing the same letter for assessment in an exam.)
- **Who** is my intended reader? For example, if you are a senior student involved in organizing a Christmas party for some local primary school kids, your letter of invitation to the children would be very different in content and style to a letter you'd send to their parents explaining the event.
- **Is the tone, style, choice of words and layout appropriate to my task?**
- **Do I need to plan my writing?** Some smaller and more informal writing tasks may be best jotted down freely. Longer and more involved tasks, such as essays and reports, need to hold together in a logical structure, so it's necessary to outline them beforehand.

How do I compose an outline?

This is similar to the technique for note-taking (see Chapter 2). First of all, **brainstorm** and write down all the ideas, opinions and information you want to use, in whatever order – just get them down on paper. Now organize your written-down thoughts. You'll probably discard some in the process, and that's OK. Then put what's left into a logical sequence and into note form. Use whatever note-taking technique suits you best:

- headings followed by step-by-step bullet points and indentations – see page 29
- memory map – see page 61
- spider graph – see page 60
- flow chart – see page 60
- or any technique that you personally find more helpful.

Your task in now broken down into steps, and that's the key to successful writing. Each step gets a new paragraph, and where possible you should use a **topic sentence**. This is a sentence, usually at the beginning of the paragraph (but sometimes at the end or even in the middle) that highlights the point the paragraph is making and everything else in the paragraph should be a development or illustration of that point.

Your first paragraph, the **introduction**, should make clear what the body of the report or essay is going to be about. (Story-writing is different from essay-writing, as the purpose of the first paragraph is usually to grip the readers and entice them to read on. This can be done by starting with an exciting incident or establishing the time, setting and characters.)

Your last paragraph, the **conclusion**, should be brief and should complete the main points of your argument and/or make a final, emphatic statement of your point of view or findings.

In between the introduction and conclusion, work your way through each paragraph in turn. A tried and tested method is to write at least three paragraphs, each one making one specific point with at least one example to illustrate that point.

Be clear about the **purpose** of your essay/assignment. If it's a **story** it should have the features one would expect in a story, such as a plot, characters and description. If it is an **informative piece** it should present all your information point-by-point. If it's a **persuasive** or **argumentative essay**, it should present your points *and* try to show weaknesses in opposing arguments.

The following formula will be useful in exams and assessments when you need to focus your mind quickly:

Introduction	State your argument/point of view briefly and clearly so no one is in any doubt where you stand.
Body	At least three paragraphs, each one giving a point in support of your argument, backed up with examples. Start with what you consider your most persuasive or strongest point and work downwards. (The theory is that if you put across your strong points first, by the time the readers gets to your weaker points

they will be almost convinced of your argument already, so may not even see your final points as 'weak'.) In one of your paragraphs you should also consider the opposing point of view and say why you disagree with it.

Conclusion   Sum up your points or argument, using strong and emphatic language.

This idea of logical sequencing is very important, as one of the examiner's main tasks is to decide whether the writing **coheres** (holds together) properly. Very often marks are lost because the student wanders off the point in mid-essay, or the whole thing is so garbled that the examiner loses track of the points being made. You can always tell when a piece of extended writing has been planned or not.

'But I can't write an outline. I can write better if I just get on with it.'

Some writers may be able to do this but they are very few and far between, and if their writing *is* coherent and logical, then they clearly have the gift of planning intuitively or subconsciously. Most people, however, need to compose an outline, and those who find it challenging have perhaps not discovered a method that works for them. Or maybe they've developed a mental block about it and just need to practise it a lot more.

It's unfortunate that writing is still the main form of

assessment in so many different subjects. As one teacher said, 'Mary has worked very hard and her Home Economics skills are well developed. It's a great pity that her written work pulled her down in the exam.'

Assessment through the written word is necessary in subjects like English, but in other subjects assessment of skills by hands-on or practical means and through the spoken word is gradually becoming more widespread. However, while reading and writing hold sway it's well worth making sure you get back to the basics if need be!

Study Tips

1. For effective reading scan the text before reading it through. Then try to read it twice – one reading is rarely enough.

2. In an exam spend time reading the paper carefully. Resist the temptation to rush at it!

3. Intelligent reading means asking questions as you go. Who? Where? When? Why? How?, etc.

4. In every writing task be clear about your purpose and intended reader. This will help you choose an appropriate format, wording and tone.

5. Before writing an essay or report, prepare an outline in your preferred form (notes, memory map, diagram, etc.). This will ensure coherence (a logical sequence of ideas).

Chapter 9

Let's Review!

The purpose of this short chapter is to review the key points made up to now. And knowing how to review is a crucial element in successful study.

Start with the following steps:

- **Check out the condition of your workplace.** Is it warm enough? Cool enough? Is there a free flow of fresh air? (Can you remember how much of the body's oxygen intake the brain requires? – 25%)
- **Is the lighting right?**
- **Do you have all the equipment you need nearby?** Nothing breaks the flow of concentration more than the frustration of having to go and search for things such as notebooks, calculators, audiotapes and so on.
- **If you need to sit down do you have a proper work surface and a chair that supports your back?**

- **What about your physical condition?** Have
  you eaten enough, for example? Some people
  like to have a snack ready and waiting for their
  break. Have you drunk enough water and do
  you have some readily at hand for 'topping up'
  while you study? The condition of your body
  can have a profound effect on your ability to
  concentrate.

Once you have checked your workspace and your
physical condition, don't forget the following vital step
that's easily ignored. It's another case of **slowing down**
in order to **speed up**:

Before studying, spend a few moments **relaxing!**
Compose yourself. Get rid of any thoughts that are
bugging you. Prepare your mind for the work ahead
with positive self-talk. *Decide* that you're going to go
about your business in a determined and organized
fashion. You're going to proceed steadily, taking
one step at a time. All your work is going to be broken
down into manageable units. You're going to be imagi-
native and flexible in your approach. And you're
going to use as many of the suggestions about accelerated learning, outlined in previous chapters, as you
can:

- Learn by looking, listening and actually getting up
  and doing things, such as experiments (in Math
  and Science), or dramatizing (historical events,
  plays, etc.).
- Make things more visual; for example, use timelines,
  flow charts, or bright colors and illustrations in
  your notes.
- Use interpersonal skills by organizing group study
  sessions where you can not only discuss, but actu-

ally teach different segments of the course to each other.

- Use music and rhythm as learning aids.
- Use your imagination to explore problems, historical events, etc.
- Have your study sessions planned in your diary and try to keep to your schedule.

Decide at this stage how long you're going to work before taking a break. The experts say that a break of five to ten minutes should be taken after every hour. Even if you don't feel like it, they say it's better in the long run to pace yourself in this way.

And what about music? You'll have experimented by now and you'll know whether music is a help or a hindrance. If it's a help, decide what to play at this stage.

The next step is to think about what it is you hope to achieve in this review session. Thinking about the **what** will suggest the **how**. According to your purpose, you might decide to review (or learn):

- **by memorizing**: facts, figures, formulae, vocabulary . . . Flip back to Chapter 4 and see the ways you can use your multiple intelligences and learning styles to memorize more easily.
- **by reading**: this could be for a variety of purposes. It could be for understanding, for example, or to gain information, or to appreciate the beauty of language – its rhythms, tones, sounds, nuances . . . Your reading could be silent or aloud. (Reading poetry and drama, etc., aloud can be a very helpful way of appreciating the language.)

- **by writing**: in note-form, using flow charts, spider graphs, etc., or in essay or report form, as discussed in Chapter 8. Some activities might require reading and writing to be combined.
- **by listening**: to discussions, lectures, foreign languages on audiotapes, CDs or whatever. (Listening to language tapes is a great way to develop the accent and rhythm of the language you're learning.)
- **by discussion**: either with another or with others, in person, by telephone or by e-mail link. This can stimulate ideas, help you gain insights, form opinions, consider alternative views, etc.
- **by viewing**: plays, musical performances, sports techniques, discussions on current affairs and world issues, works of art or the sciences on tapes, DVDs, TV or on CD-ROMs.

REMINDER!

Despite modern advances in technology and the media, some students and their parents are still under the impression that study and review sessions have to be nose-in-book or pen-on-paper. This is not true. By using the full range of media you can exercise more of your eight intelligences (as discussed in Chapter 4) and so accelerate the learning process.

Study Tips

1. Regular review of the topics you have studied is vital. Yet it is so easily neglected!

Let's Review!

2. Check and prepare your study environment.

3. There are lots of ways to review, including reading, writing, listening, viewing, discussing, dramatising . . .

4. Regular review will really build up confidence for exams.

Chapter 10

More on Those Exams!

Chapter 6 covered the use of study timetables to help prepare for exams. Now let's look at how to maintain a positive state of mind during an exam. Never overlook the importance of this! There are many cases of able, dedicated students who have failed exams because they *allowed* their nerves to get the better of them. Like everything else, staying calm is something that has to be worked at, and some have to do this more than others. Earlier we looked at breathing and other ways of staying calm (see Chapter 5), and this chapter looks at examples of other practical things you can do.

Seen it, done it!

One of the best ways to cope with pre-exam nerves is to make yourself as familiar as possible with the procedures involved. 'Nerves' are caused by fear of the unknown, so the more you acquaint yourself with what is going to happen the better. (Some go further into panic

113

the more they find out about exams, but studying and preparing really well beforehand and making sure that the courses being taken are the best for you should be a great help.)

Exam tips that will really help

Exams can take the form of multiple choice, written assignments or both.

Multiple choice questions may seem easy, but they can be tricky. More than one answer may seem to be right. Try eliminating the wrong answers first. Make sure you choose the one that is most correct.

Exams that require written answers may seem more complicated, but there are some tried-and-true steps that will help.

- skim all parts of a question before you try to answer it
- underline important words, ideas or information
- use the space provided for an answer as a clue to the approximate length of answer expected

When writing any exam, the most important thing is not to panic. Make sure you understand the question. If you find a word you don't understand, look for a root word that you know. Or look for clues to its meaning by reading to the end of the sentence or selection. If the sentence is long and you get confused, try putting it into your own words.

How do I deal with pre-exam nerves?

An effective way to deal with pre-exam nerves is a to do a trial run of a typical test and procedures. The vice principal in a school that used a practice test with students says:

Many of our students used to dread going into an exam. In fact, it wasn't uncommon for some of them to get sick or burst into tears. You'd have thought they were going in to be tortured.

So we hit on an idea which dramatically improved the situation. We decided to use old exams to practice not just exams, but strict exam procedures. Students were going to get a taste of the real thing. I'm glad to say it really paid off.

Karen, one of the students who benefited from this, explains why:

We used to dread exams because we didn't know what to expect. But doing a practice test really helped. By the time we got to the actual exam, we'd been through the procedures and some possible questions several times. You knew what to expect. By the time we actually wrote our exam, it was no big deal. We'd seen it all before.

What else can you do?

You can become familiar with all kinds of exams. Get as much practice as possible by doing past exam papers and keeping rigorously to the time allowed. The more familiar you are with the format and time schedule of an exam, the more relaxed you'll feel when the time comes.

Why not try **relaxation** followed by **mental rehearsal**? First of all slow your mind and body down by going through a deep breathing routine. Play some quiet background music. (This can help, but it's not absolutely necessary.) After a while, when you're feeling very calm, start visualizing yourself writing the exam. In your mind's eye *see* yourself at your desk and *feel* the upbeat, optimistic frame of mind you intend to have. Tell yourself that no matter what surprises the paper may have in store, you're going to stay calm and tackle each question positively and optimistically. Do this regularly, then when you approach the exam in reality go through your breathing routine. Your mind will automatically switch on to the positive feelings. You may see some students desperately trying to cram facts and figures into their heads right up to the last minute. This only raises stress levels; have faith in your preparation, and you will be in a much better position to bring out your best.

It is important to keep both negative thoughts and negative talk at bay. This is a lesson Billy learned too late:

I felt quite good about my exam until I met my friends at school. Some of the girls used to talk about how hard it was going to be and how sick they felt and how we weren't going to have enough time. The boys didn't say very much but you could always tell by their faces they were worried. By the time we went in for the exam we all felt pretty miserable . . . I know I could have done much better.

Picking up negative vibes is a natural human tendency, but what can you do to overcome it when it's more or less in your face? Use the power of your imagination! Famous sprinter Linford Christie used to come up against people trying to worry and distract him before major races in an attempt to put him off. Christie says he used to imagine himself enclosed in a bubble; no negative energy from outside could get in, leaving him free to focus his mind on winning and nothing else. You can do the same! Block it out, imagine yourself surrounded by an invisible wall, so that any negative talk you hear just bounces off. Smile to yourself and send out positive thoughts for anyone who needs them. Try to keep your language positive as well, both in your thoughts and when speaking to others. That way, unlike Billy, you'll stay calm.

Language

Have you noticed the language people use when they try to be helpful? How many times have you heard someone say, 'Don't panic!' – and immediately you start to feel nervous? That's the power of negative language. Get into the habit of expressing the same ideas in a positive way. Say 'Stay calm' instead of 'Don't Panic!' *You* can be the one to set the tone of conversations before exams, and you'll do yourself and everyone else a favor.

Once you're under way . . .

Having kept your cool, gotten yourself through the door and allowed your mental rehearsal programming to kick in, it's now time to write the exam. Make the workspace your own. Organize your pens, pencils and other equipment. Bring in something that reminds you of your familiar workspace (check to make sure what the rules are for materials you can take into an exam). This also helps you to feel relaxed.

Timing

It's a very good idea to put your watch in front of you, even if there's a large clock at the front of the hall. Glancing at your watch every now and then will remind you to pace yourself.

Allow a few minutes to look through the paper in a relaxed way. Select the parts you are going to answer and estimate how long you should take for each section. Try to keep to your schedule. It may not work out exactly, but by attempting to manage your time you will avoid a fairly common mistake: spending far too much time on one section at the expense of others.

What should you do if you accidentally miss a page or find you're just running out of time?

Michelle found herself in that position in one of her exams and she did exactly the right thing:

> *I added a note! Not a real note – just a few words in the margin explaining, 'No time left but here's what I would have written'. I had jotted down an outline in rough note-form of the points I would have covered. When the papers were returned I was delighted to see that at least I got a few marks for my attempt. But guess what. That couple of marks made the difference between a pass and fail grade, so I didn't have to re-write the exam.*

This sort of thing can impress teachers. After all, an exam is not meant to be a trap, it's a chance for you to display your knowledge, understanding or skills. If, like Michelle, you can show that you have understood the question and can go some of the way towards answering it, chances are you'll be given some credit.

And finally: enjoy yourself!

Students often find this difficult to believe, but you can *enjoy* exams! If you've chosen the right courses, worked well, have kept yourself fit both mentally and physically and have made good progress, there's no reason why you shouldn't approach your exams confidently and optimistically. See them as an opportunity to show what you can do. Enjoy the challenge!

The advice in this book is intended as material to get you going, in a positive, upward direction. It is by no means exhaustive. And you might find you don't agree with it all. Different things work for different people, and it's up to you to experiment and discover what works best for you. Think carefully about your studies and how your lifestyle (your leisure activities, your home life, your school life and your attitude) can have a bearing on your progress. Above all, keep things in perspective. Find that comfortable balance between your studies and the other areas of your life, and you'll shine.

Good luck, and may you get the grades your hard work deserves!

Study Tips

1. In the build-up to exams some people stay calm naturally – but most of us have to work at it!

2. Becoming familiar with all aspects of the exam will help.

3. Practise relaxing and visualizing success in your exams.

4. Avoid negative talk and negative body language from others. Keep your own language and demeanor positive.

More on Those Exams!

5. *Once your exams are under way try to stay calm and organized.*

6. *Keep an eye on the clock – timing is important.*

7. *If you run out of time or realize you have missed a page/question – write a brief outline of the points you would have made.*

Index

Index

Index

Acknowledgments

Thanks to Norma Black for permission to cite her school resource *The Learning Game*.

And many thanks to Brenda and Yasemin at Piccadilly Press for their very helpful suggestions and support.

Author's note

All stories and indicidents described in this book are based on real-life events and interviews, although in some cases names and situations have been changed. Permission to recount experiences have been obtained from all involved.